A-Z Street Atlas of ALDERSHOT and District

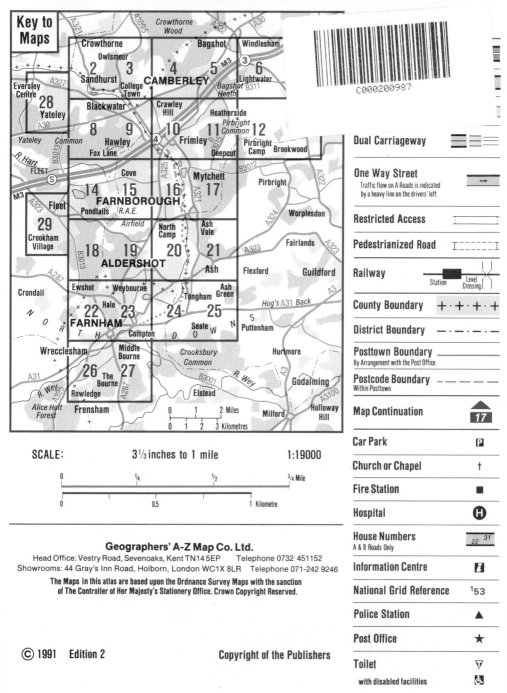

C000200987

Key to Maps

Crowthorne Wood · Crowthorne · Owlsmoor · Bagshot · Windlesham · 2 · 3 · 4 · 5 · 6 · Sandhurst · College Town · CAMBERLEY · Bagshot Heath · Lightwater · B311 · Eversley Centre · 28 Yateley · Blackwater · Crawley Hill · Heatherside · 8 · 9 · 10 · 11 · 12 · Yateley Common · Hawley · Fox Lane · Frimley · Pirbright Common · Pirbright Camp · Brookwood · Deepcut · R. Hart · FLEET · Cove · Mytchett · Pirbright · 14 · 15 · 16 · 17 · FARNBOROUGH · Pondtails · R.A.E. · Worplesdon · Fleet · 29 · Crookham Village · Airfield · North Camp · Ash Vale · Fairlands · 18 · 19 · 20 · 21 · ALDERSHOT · Ash · Flexford · Guildford · Crondall · Ewshot · Weybourne · Tongham · Ash Green · Hog's Back · 22 · 23 · 24 · 25 · Hale · FARNHAM · Compton · Seale · Puttenham · Wrecclesham · Middle Bourne · Crooksbury Common · Hurtmore · 26 · 27 · The Bourne · Elstead · Godalming · Rowledge · Frensham · Milford · Holloway Hill · Alice Holt Forest

0 1 2 Miles
0 1 2 3 Kilometres

SCALE: 3⅓ inches to 1 mile 1:19000

0 · ¼ · ½ · ¾ Mile
0 · 0.5 · 1 Kilometre

Legend

Symbol	Meaning
Dual Carriageway	
One Way Street — Traffic flow on A Roads is indicated by a heavy line on the drivers' left	→
Restricted Access	
Pedestrianized Road	
Railway	Station / Level Crossing
County Boundary	+ + + +
District Boundary	— · — · —
Posttown Boundary — By Arrangement with the Post Office	
Postcode Boundary — Within Posttown	— — —
Map Continuation	17
Car Park	P
Church or Chapel	†
Fire Station	■
Hospital	H
House Numbers — A & B Roads Only	22 31
Information Centre	i
National Grid Reference	¹53
Police Station	▲
Post Office	★
Toilet	▽
with disabled facilities	♿

Geographers' A-Z Map Co. Ltd.

Head Office: Vestry Road, Sevenoaks, Kent TN14 5EP   Telephone 0732 451152
Showrooms: 44 Gray's Inn Road, Holborn, London WC1X 8LR   Telephone 071-242 9246

The Maps in this atlas are based upon the Ordnance Survey Maps with the sanction of The Controller of Her Majesty's Stationery Office. Crown Copyright Reserved.

© 1991   Edition 2   Copyright of the Publishers

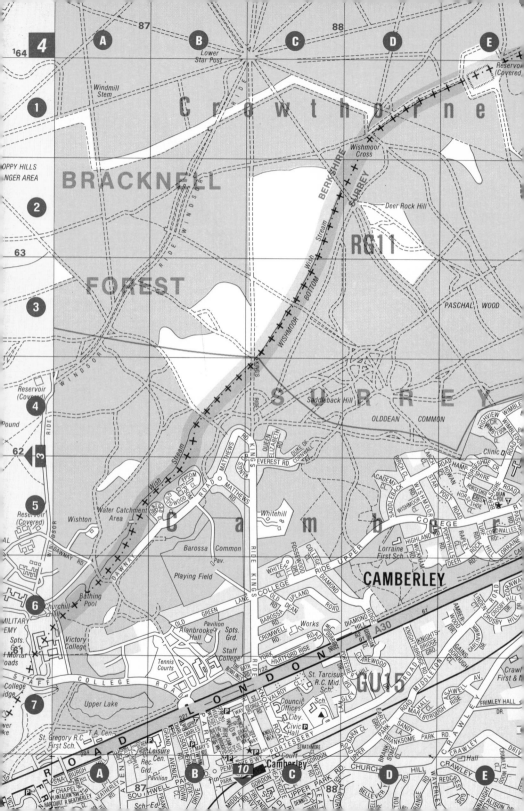

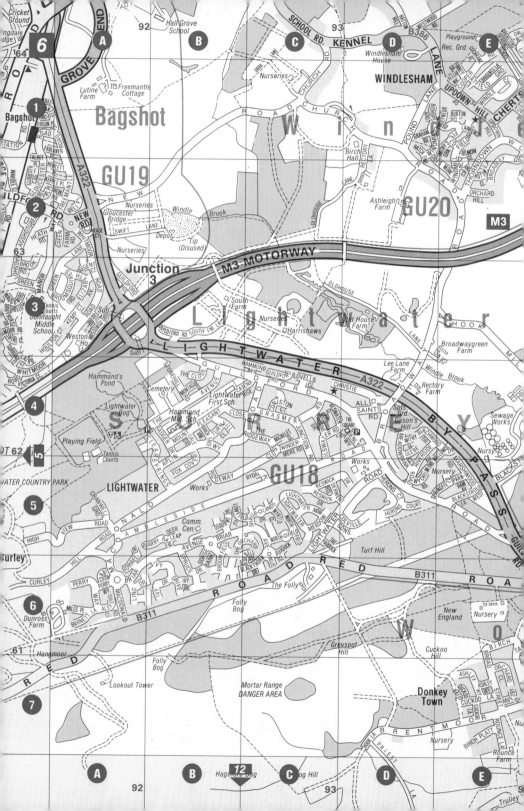

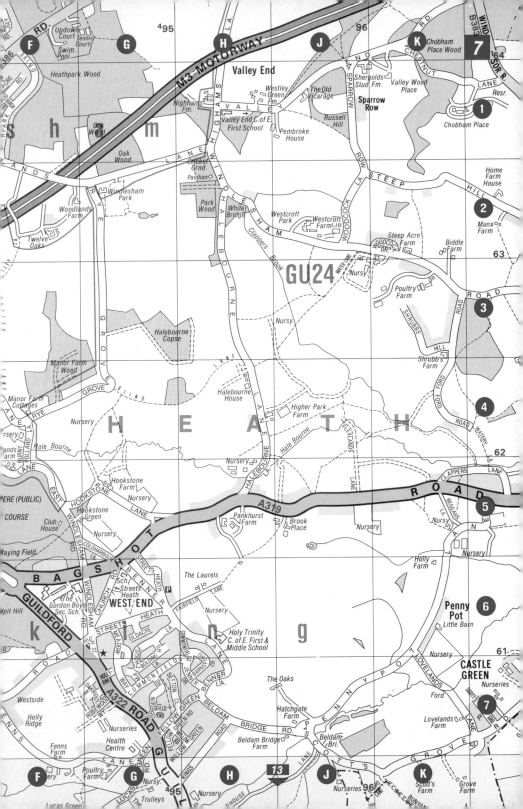

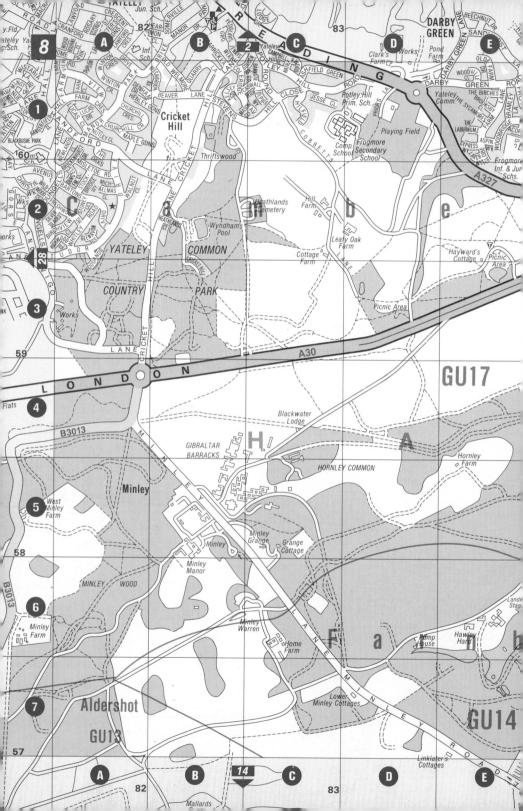

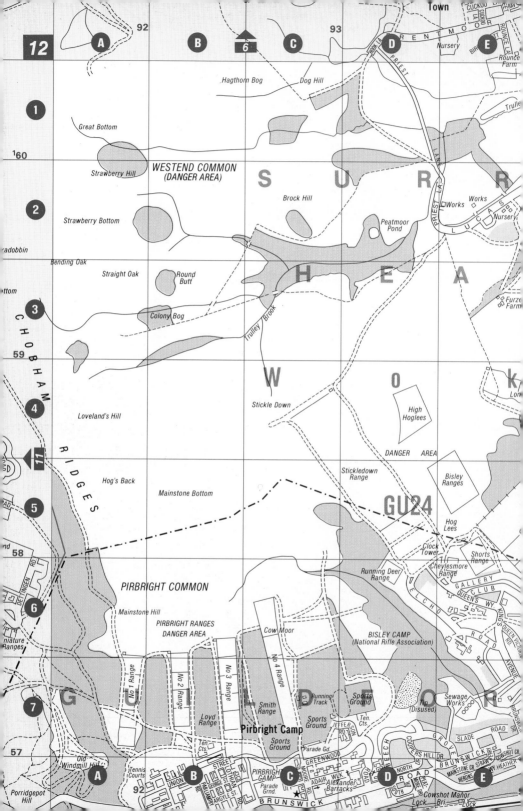

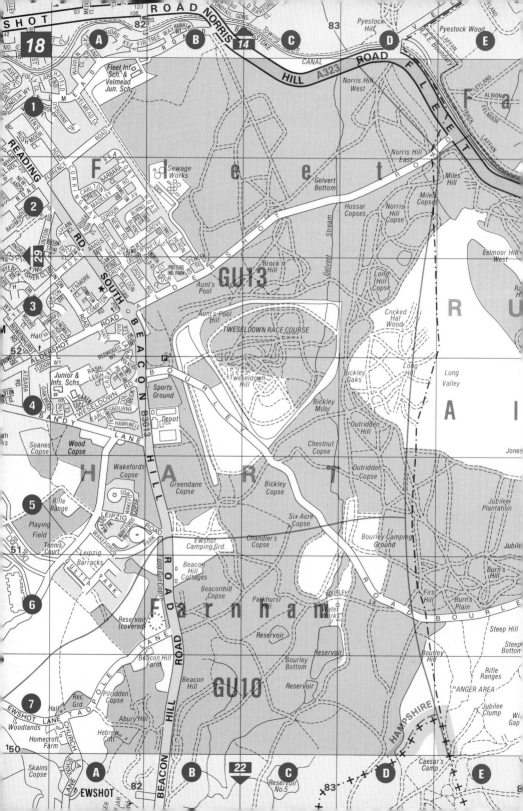

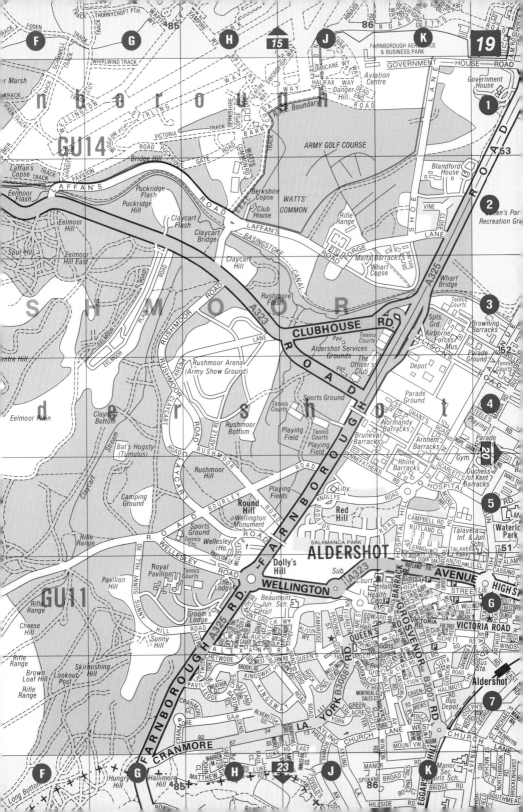

INDEX TO STREETS

HOW TO USE THIS INDEX

(a) A strict alphabetical order is followed in which Av., Rd., St., etc. are read in full and as part of the name preceding them; e.g. Apple Tree Way. follows Applelands Clo. but precedes Approach Rd.
(b) Each street is followed by its Postal Code District Number and map reference; e.g. Abbetts La. GU15—3A 10 is in the Guildford 15 Postal Code District and is to be found in square 3A on page 10.

N.B. The Postal Code District Numbers given in this index are, in fact, only the first part of the Postcode to each address and are only meant to indicate the Postal Code District in which each street is situated.

ABBREVIATIONS USED IN THIS INDEX

All : Alley	Clo : Close	Gt : Great	Mkt : Market	Rd : Road
App : Approach	Comn : Common	Grn : Green	M : Mews	S : South
Arc : Arcade	Cotts : Cottages	Gro : Grove	Mt : Mount	Sq : Square
Av : Avenue	Ct : Court	GU : Guildford	N : North	Sta : Station
Bk : Back	Cres : Crescent	Ho : House	Pal : Palace	St : Street
Boulevd : Boulevard	Dri : Drive	Ind : Industrial	Pde : Parade	Ter : Terrace
Bri : Bridge	E : East	Junct : Junction	Pk : Park	Up : Upper
B'way : Broadway	Embkmt : Embankment	La : Lane	Pas : Passage	Vs : Villas
Bldgs : Buildings	Est : Estate	Lit : Little	Pl : Place	Wlk : Walk
Chyd : Churchyard	Gdns : Gardens	Lwr : Lower	Prom : Promenade	W : West
Cir : Circus	Ga : Gate	Mans : Mansions	RG : Reading	Yd : Yard

Abbetts La. GU15—3A 10
Abbey Ct. GU9—7F 23
Abbey Ct. GU15—1C 10
Abbey St. GU9—7F 23
Abbey Way. GU14—3B 16
Abbots Clo. GU13—2K 29
Abbot's Ride. GU9—2H 27
Abercorn Ho. GU17—5H 9
Abingdon Rd. GU17—5F 3
Acacia Av. GU15—4G 3
Academy Clo. GU15—5D 4
Acheulian Clo. GU9—3F 27
Ackrells Mead. GU17—4C 2
Acorn M. GU14—7K 9
Acorn Rd. GU17—1E 8
Adair Wlk. GU24—7C 12
Adams Dri. GU13—6B 14
Adams Pk. Rd. GU9—5G 23
Addiscombe Rd. RG11—1F 3
Adlington Pl. GU14—5D 16
Admiralty Way. GU15—2J 9
Ainger Clo. GU12—5C 20
Aircraft Esplanade. GU14
　　　　　—6B 16
Aisne Rd. GU16—5K 11
Alamein Rd. GU11—6A 20
Alanbrooke Rd. GU11—2C 20
Albany Clo. GU13—7A 14
Albany Ct. GU13—6A 14
Albany Pk. GU15—5B 10
Albany Rd. GU13—3K 29
Albert Rd. GU11—6A 20
Albert Rd. GU14—5B 16
Albert Rd. GU19—4K 5
Albert Rd. RG11—1E 2
Albert St. GU13—3J 29
Albion Rd. GU17—5E 2
Albury Cotts. GU12—6H 21
Alcot Clo. RG11—1E 2
Alderbrook Clo. RG11—1B 2
Alder Clo. GU12—1F 21
Alder Gro. GU17—4E 28
Aldershot Lodge. GU11—1K 23
Aldershot Rd. GU12—1D 24
Aldershot Rd. GU13—7J 29
　　(Church Crookham)
Aldershot Rd. GU13—3K 29
　　(Fleet)
Alders, The. GU13—6H 29
Aldrin Pl. GU14—3G 15
Aldwick Clo. GU14—1K 9
Alexandra Av. GU15—1K 9
Alexandra Ct. GU14—6B 16
Alexandra Rd. GU11—6H 19
Alexandra Rd. GU12—7E 20
Alexandra Rd. GU14—5B 16
Alfonso Clo. GU12—1B 24
Alfred Rd. GU9—1F 27
Alfriston Rd. GU16—7H 11
Alice Rd. GU11—6A 20
Alison Clo. GU14—4J 15
Alison Dri. GU15—1E 10

Alison's Rd. GU11—3K 19
Alison Way. GU11—6J 19
Allden Av. GU12—2C 24
Allden Gdns. GU12—2C 24
Allenby Rd. GU15—7K 3
Allendale Clo. GU17—3D 2
All Saints Clo. GU14—5H 9
All Saints Rd. GU18—4D 6
Alma Clo. GU12—6C 20
Alma Cotts. GU14—7B 16
Alma La. GU9—2E 22
Alma Sq. GU14—7B 16
Alma Way. GU9—2G 23
Almond Ct. GU13—7A 14
Aloes, The. GU13—7A 14
Alphington Av. GU16—5D 10
Alphington Grn. GU16—5E 10
Alsace Wlk. GU15—5A 10
Alsford Clo. GU18—6A 6
Alton Ride. GU17—7F 3
Alton Rd. GU10—4A 26
Alton Rd. GU13—6B 14
Alverstoke Gdns. GU11—7H 19
Ambarrow Cres. GU17—4C 2
Ambarrow La. GU17—3A 2
Amberley Grange. GU11—1J 23
Amberwood Dri. GU15—6E 4
Ambleside Clo. GU14—3H 15
Ambleside Clo. GU16—5F 17
Ambleside Cres. GU9—3D 22
Ambleside Rd. GU18—5A 6
Amity Way. GU15—1D 10
Ancells Business Pk. GU13
　　　　　—2A 14
Ancells Rd. GU13—3A 14
Anchor Cres. GU21—4K 13
Anchor Hill. GU21—4K 13
Anchor Meadow. GU14—3J 15
Anderson Pl. GU19—1K 5
Andover Rd. GU17—7F 3
Andover Way. GU11—2A 24
Andrewartha Rd. GU14—5D 16
Andrews Clo. GU13—5K 29
Andrews Rd. GU14—2H 15
Angelica Rd. GU24—2H 13
Anglesey Av. GU14—7J 9
Anglesey Rd. GU12—7C 20
Angora Way. GU13—3A 14
Annandale Dri. GU10—4G 27
Annes Way. GU13—2A 18
Ansell Rd. GU16—6D 10
Anzio Clo. GU11—6K 19
Apex Dri. GU16—5C 10
Aplin Way. GU18—5B 6
Apollo Rise. GU14—3G 15
Appledore M. GU14—7K 9
Applelands Clo. GU10—6D 26
Apple Tree Way. GU15—4G 3
Appley Ct. GU15—1A 10
Appley Dri. GU15—7A 4
Approach Rd. GU15—1F 27
April Clo. GU15—4B 10

Arcade, The. GU11—6K 19
Ardrossan Av. GU15—2F 11
Ardwell Clo. RG11—1B 2
Arena La. GU11—4G 19
Arenal Dri. RG11—2E 2
Arethusa Way. GU24—3G 13
Argents Clo. GU13—3A 14
Argyle St. GU24—7B 12
Arlington Ter. GU11—6J 19
Armitage Dri. GU16—5E 10
Armstrong Mall. GU14—3G 15
Arnhem Barracks. GU11—4K 19
Arnhem Clo. GU11—6A 20
Arrow Rd. GU14—5J 15
Arthur Clo. GU9—1E 26
Arthur Clo. GU9—4K 5
Arthur Rd. GU9—1E 26
　　(in two parts)
Arthur St. GU11—6A 20
Artillery Rd. GU11—6A 20
Arundel Clo. GU13—7A 14
Arundel Pl. GU9—7E 22
Arundel Rd. GU15—2H 11
Ashbourne Clo. GU12—5H 21
Ashbury Dri. GU17—5K 9
Ash Chu. Rd. GU12—6G 21
Ash Clo. GU12—5G 21
Ash Clo. GU17—1F 9
Ash Ct. GU11—5K 19
Ashdene Cres. GU12—5F 21
Ashdene Rd. GU12—5F 21
Ashdown Av. GU14—5C 16
Ashfield Grn. GU17—1C 8
Ash Grn. La. E. GU12—1H 25
Ash Grn. La. W. GU10 & GU12
　　　　　—1E 24
Ash Grn. Rd. GU12—7H 21
Ash Hill Rd. GU12—4F 21
Ashley Clo. GU16—1F 17
Ashley Dri. GU17—2F 9
Ashley Rd. GU14—3C 16
Ashley Way. GU24—7E 6
Ash Lodge Clo. GU12—7F 21
Ash Lodge Dri. GU12—7E 20
Ashridge. GU14—7J 9
Ash Rd. GU12—7B 20
Ash St. GU12—7E 20
Ash Tree Clo. GU14—4F 15
Ashurst Rd. GU12—4F 21
Ashwell Av. GU15—7E 4
Aspin Way. GU17—1E 8
Atbara Rd. GU13—7K 29
Atfield Gro. GU20—1E 6
Atrebatti Rd. GU17—4F 3
Attenborough Clo. GU13
　　　　　—4B 14
Attfield Clo. GU12—7E 20
Attlee Gdns. GU13—7J 29
Auchinleck Way. GU11—6H 19
Augustus Gdns. GU15—1H 11
Austen Rd. GU14—1K 15
Aveley Clo. GU9—3F 27

Aveley La. GU9—4E 26
Avenue Rd. GU13—1J 29
Avenue Rd. GU14—3C 16
Avenue Sucy. GU15—2A 10
Avenue, The. GU10—6C 26
Avenue, The. GU12—2C 24
Avenue, The. GU13—2H 29
Avenue, The. GU15—1A 10
Avenue, The. GU18—4B 6
Avocet Cres. GU15—5G 3
Avon Clo. GU12—7E 20
Avon Clo. GU14—7H 9
Avon Ct. GU9—1F 27
Avondale. GU12—1E 20
Avondale Rd. GU11—1A 24
Avondale Rd. GU13—1K 29
Avon Rd. GU9—1F 27
Award Rd. GU13—6K 29
Aylesham Way. GU17—3D 28
Ayling Ct. GU9—2J 23
Ayling Hill. GU11—7J 19
Ayling La. GU11—1J 23
Ayrshire Gdns. GU13—3A 14
Azalea Way. GU15—7G 5

Babbs Mead. GU9—1D 26
Bacon Clo. GU15—6G 3
Badajos Rd. GU11—5J 19
Badger Dri. GU18—4B 6
Badgers Clo. GU13—3J 29
Badgers Copse. GU15—3D 10
Badgers Holt. GU17—4D 28
Badger Way. GU10—1A 22
Badgerwood Dri. GU16—4C 10
Badshot Lea Rd. GU9—4J 23
Badshot Pk. GU9—3K 23
Bagshot Grn. GU19—2K 5
Bagshot Rd. GU21, GU24, GU22
　　　　　& GU3—5J 13
Bagshot Rd. GU24—6F 7
Baigents La. GU20—1E 6
Bailey Clo. GU16—6C 10
Baileys Clo. GU17—2F 9
Bain Av. GU15—4A 10
Baird Rd. GU14—1B 16
Baldreys. GU9—2D 26
Balintore Ct. GU15—5G 3
Ballantyne Rd. GU14—1K 15
Ballard Ct. GU15—5F 5
Ballard Rd. GU15—5F 5
Balliol Way. GU15—4H 3
Ball & Wicket La. GU9—6F 23
Balmoral Cres. GU9—3E 22
Balmoral Dri. GU16—6D 10
Balmoral Rd. GU12—4F 21
Banbury Clo. GU16—7E 10
Bankside. GU9—2J 23
Bannister Gdns. GU17—1C 8
Barbara Clo. GU13—2A 18
Barberry Clo. GU13—5K 29
Barberry Way. GU17—4J 9

Barbon Clo. GU15—3J 11
Bardsley Dri. GU9—2D 26
Barford Clo. GU13—7C 14
Barkis Mead. GU15—3H 3
Barley Mow Clo. GU21—4K 13
Barley Mow La. GU21—3K 13
Barley Way. GU13—2A 14
Barnard Clo. GU16—6E 10
Barn Clo. GU15—7D 4
Barnes Clo. GU14—3C 16
Barnes Rd. GU16—6D 10
Barnett La. GU18—6A 6
Barnsford Cres. GU24—7H 7
Barnsley Clo. GU12—5G 17
Barossa Rd. GU15—6C 4
Barracane Dri. RG11—1D 2
Barrack Rd. GU11—6K 19
Barrie Rd. GU9—2D 22
Barr's La. GU21—3K 13
Barton Clo. GU11—7H 19
Bartons Dri. GU17—2A 8
Basingbourne Clo. GU13
　　　　　—5K 29
Basingbourne Rd. GU13—6J 29
Basing Dri. GU11—2A 24
Basset Clo. GU16—6D 10
Bat & Ball La. GU10—4D 26
　　(in two parts)
Bath Rd. GU15—7C 4
Bayfield Av. GU16—4C 10
Bayford Clo. GU17—5K 9
Beacon Clo. GU10—5D 26
Beacon Gdns. GU13—2H 29
Beacon Hill Rd. GU13 & GU10
　　　　　—3A 18
Beales La. GU10—3C 26
Beam Hollow. GU9—2F 23
Bear La. GU9—6E 22
Bearwood Gdns. GU13—2K 29
Beaufort Rd. GU9—6F 23
Beaufort Rd. GU13—2A 18
Beaufront Clo. GU16—4C 10
Beaufront Rd. GU15—6F 5
Beaulieu Gdns. GU17—1F 9
Beaumont Gro. GU11—6H 19
Beaver La. GU17—1B 8
Beavers Clo. GU9—7D 22
Beavers Hill. GU9—7C 22
Beavers Rd. GU9—7D 22
Beck Gdns. GU9—3E 22
Bedford Av. GU16—7D 10
Bedford Cres. GU16—1D 16
Bedford La. GU16—1E 16
Beech Av. GU10—5F 27
Beech Av. GU15—2C 10
Beechbrook Av. GU17—1B 8
Beech Clo. GU11—6K 19
Beeches, The. GU9—2G 9
Beeches, The. GU17—7E 16
Beech Farm La. GU15—2E 10
Beech Gro. GU24—7D 12
Beeching Clo. GU12—5G 21

Beechnut Dri. GU17—7E 2
Beechnut Rd. GU12—7A 20
Beech Ride. GU13—4J 29
Beech Ride. GU17—5E 2
Beech Rd. GU14—7K 9
Beech Rd. GU16—1E 16
Beech Tree Dri. GU04—4K 23
Beech Wlk. GU20—1E 6
Beechwood Clo. GU13—5H 29
Beeton's Av. GU12—4F 21
Beggars La. GU24—5K 7
Beldam Bri. Rd. GU24—7H 7
Beldham Rd. GU9—3C 26
Belgrave Ct. GU17—3G 9
Belland Dri. GU11—7H 19
Bell Clo. GU14—1B 16
Belle View Rd. GU12—6C 20
Belle Vue Clo. GU12—6C 20
Bellew Rd. GU16—1G 17
Bellingham Clo. GU15—2H 11
Bell La. GU10—7B 26
Bell La. GU17—1F 9
Bell Pl. GU19—2A 6
Belmont Clo. GU14—7J 9
Belmont M. GU15—3B 10
Belmont Rd. GU15—2B 10
Belstone M. GU14—7K 9
Belton Rd. GU15—1D 10
Belvedere Clo. GU13—2F 29
Belvedere Ct. GU17—3G 9
Belvedere Rd. GU14—5B 16
Belvoir Clo. GU16—5E 10
Benner La. GU24—6G 7
Bennet Ct. GU15—1B 10
Benson Rd. RG11—1C 2
Benwell Rd. GU24—6G 13
Beresford Clo. GU14—6F 11
Berkeley Clo. GU13—6A 14
Berkeley Cres. GU16—6F 11
Berkshire Rd. GU15—5E 4
Bernard Ct. GU15—2A 10
Bernersh Clo. GU17—4F 3
Berrybank. GU15—7H 3
Beta Rd. GU14—2J 15
Bethel Clo. GU9—3G 23
Bethel La. GU9—7F 23
Betjeman Wlk. GU17—5D 28
Beveren Clo. GU13—3A 14
Beverley Clo. GU12—7E 20
Beverley Clo. GU15—7J 5
Beverley Cres. GU14—7C 15
Bicknell Rd. GU16—4D 10
Bideford Clo. GU14—7K 9
Binstead Copse. GU13—4J 29
Binstead Rd. GU17—1G 9
Binton La. GU10—7D 24
Birch Av. GU13—1J 29
Birch Clo. GU10—6D 26
Birch Clo. GU15—5D 4
Birch Ct. GU13—1J 29
Birch Dri. GU17—3G 9
Birches, The. GU14—3G 15
Birches, The. GU17—1E 8
Birchett Rd. GU11—6K 19
Birchett Rd. GU14—2H 15
Birchfields. GU15—2B 10
Birch La. GU24—6E 6
Birch Pde. GU13—2J 29
Birch Rd. GU20—1F 7
Birch Tree View. GU18—4B 6
Birchview Clo. GU17—5E 28
Birch Way. GU12—1F 21
Birchwood Dri. GU18—4D 6
Birdhaven. GU10—4D 26
Birdsgrove. GU15—5J 13
Birdwood Rd. GU15—6J 3
Birkbeck Pl. GU15—4H 3
Bishops Clo. GU13—5K 29
Bishops Gro. GU20—1D 6
Bishops Mead. GU19—7E 22
Bishops Rd. GU9—2E 22
Bishop Sumner Dri. GU9—3F 23
Bittern Clo. GU15—5G 3
Blackbird Clo. GU15—5G 3

Blackbushe Airport. GU17
—6D 28
Blackbushe Business Pk. GU17
—6E 28
Blackbushe Pk. GU17—4E 28
Blackcap Pl. GU15—5H 3
Blackdown Barracks. GU16
—7J 11
(off Brunswick Rd.)
Blackdown Barracks. GU16
—6K 11
(off Newfoundland Rd.)
Blackdown Rd. GU16—7H 11
Blackheath Rd. GU9—2D 22
Black Pond La. GU10—4F 27
Blackstone Clo. GU14—1G 15
Blackstroud La. E. GU18—5E 6
Blackstroud La. W. GU18—5E 6
Blackthorn Cres. GU14—6J 9
Blackthorn Dri. GU18—6C 6
Blackwater Clo. GU12—7F 21
Blackwater Ind. Est. GU17
—1H 9
Blackwater Valley Relief Rd.
GU15—2J 9
Blackwater Way. GU12—1C 24
Blaire Pk. GU17—1D 28
Blaise Clo. GU14—4C 16
Blake Clo. RG11—1F 3
(Crowthorne)
Blakes Ride. GU17—3D 28
Bleitigheim Way. GU15—7B 4
Blenheim Clo. GU10—2D 24
Blenheim Ct. GU14—5C 16
Blenheim Cres. GU9—4D 22
Blenheim Pk. GU11—1B 20
Blenheim Rd. GU11—1B 20
Blighton La. GU10—6C 24
Blind La. GU24—4G 7
Bloomsbury Way. GU17—3F 9
Bluebell Rise. GU18—6C 6
Bluebell Wlk. GU15—1J 29
Bluethroat Clo. GU15—5H 3
Bluff Cove. GU11—5B 20
Blunden Rd. GU14—3J 15
Blythwood Dri. GU16—4C 10
Bolding Ho. La. GU24—7G 7
Borderside. GU17—3C 28
Borelli M. GU9—7F 23
Borelli Yd. GU9—7F 23
Borough, The. GU9—7F 22
Borrowdale Gdns. GU15—1J 11
Botany Hill. GU10—7C 24
Boulter's Rd. GU11—6A 20
Boundary Rd. GU11—7B 26
Boundary Rd. GU14—5B 16
Boundary Vs. GU17—2H 9
Boundstone Clo. GU10—5E 26
Boundstone Rd. GU10—6C 26
Bourley La. GU10—6C 18
Bourley Rd. GU13, GU10 & GU11
—4B 18
Bourne Ct. GU11—1K 23
Bourne Dene. GU10—5D 26
Bourne Firs. GU10—5G 27
Bourne Gro. GU10—3H 27
Bourne Gro. Clo. GU10—3H 27
Bourne Gro. GU10—3H 27
Bourne, The. GU13—5K 29
Bowenhurst Gdns. GU13
—6K 29
Bowenhurst Rd. GU13—6K 29
Bower Rd. GU10—5D 26
Bowling Grn. Ct. GU16—7D 10
Bowlings, The. GU15—7B 4
Boxall's Gro. GU11—2K 23
Boxall's La. GU11—2K 23
Brabon Rd. GU14—2J 15
Bracebridge. GU15—1K 9
Brackendale Clo. GU15—3D 10
Brackendale Rd. GU15—1C 10
Brackendene. GU12—5H 21
Bracken La. GU17—3C 28
Bracklesham Clo. GU14—7K 9
Bracknell Clo. GU15—4E 4
Bracknell Rd. GU15—3F 5
Braemar Clo. GU16—6E 10

Brakenwood. GU15—1J 11
Bramblebank. GU16—1F 17
Brambleton Av. GU9—2E 26
Bramblewood Pl. GU13—2H 29
Bramcote. GU15—1H 11
Bramley Ct. RG11—1B 2
Bramley Ct. GU17—1E 8
Bramley Rd. GU15—4A 10
Bramling Av. GU17—3D 28
Bramshot Dri. GU13—1K 29
Bramshott La. GU13 & GU14
—3D 14
Brandon Clo. GU15—2J 11
Branksome Clo. GU15—7D 4
Branksome Ct. GU13—2J 29
Branksome Hill Rd. GU15—6H 3
Branksome Pk. Rd. GU15—7D 4
Branksomewood Rd. GU13
—1H 29
Braye Clo. GU17—4F 3
Brecon Clo. GU17—7G 9
Brendon Rd. GU14—7G 9
Brentmoor Rd. GU24—7D 6
Brethart Rd. GU16—5D 10
Brewers Clo. GU14—3K 15
Briar Av. GU18—6A 6
Briarleas Ct. GU14—7C 16
Briars Clo. GU14—4G 15
Brickfield Cotts. RG11—2C 2
Bricksbury. GU9—2F 23
Bridge End. GU15—2A 10
Bridgefield. GU9—7G 23
Bridgemead. GU16—6B 10
Bridge Rd. GU11—1K 23
Bridge Rd. GU14—3J 15
Bridge Rd. GU15—3A 10
Bridge Rd. GU19—2K 5
Bridge Sq. GU9—7F 23
Bridge Wlk. GU17—6A 2
Bridle Ct. GU11—6H 19
Brighton Rd. GU12—1B 24
Brightwells Rd. GU9—7F 23
Brindle Clo. GU11—2A 24
Brinksway. GU13—3K 29
Brinn's La. GU17—1F 9
Bristow Cres. GU15—3B 10
Bristow Rd. GU15—3A 10
Brittain Ct. GU17—6F 3
Brittens Clo. GU12—6G 21
Broadacres. GU13—3G 29
Broad Ha'penny. GU10—6D 26
Broadhurst. GU14—3F 15
Broadlands. GU14—5D 16
Broadlands. GU16—6E 10
Broadley Grn. GU20—2E 6
Broadmoor Est. RG11—1G 3
Broad Oaks. GU11—1K 23
Broad St. GU24—6E 6
Broad Wlk. GU16—4D 10
Broadway. GU21—5J 13
(Knaphill)
Broadway Ct. GU21—4K 13
Broadway Rd. GU18 & GU20
—4D 6
Broadway, The. GU17—5E 2
Broadwell Rd. GU10—4C 26
Brockenhurst Dri. GU17—2A 8
Brockenhurst Rd. GU11—1A 24
Brocklands. GU17—7H 9
Bromley Ct. GU15—1G 27
Brook Av. GU9—2J 23
Brook Clo. GU12—5G 21
Brook Clo. GU15—4H 3
Brook Cotts. GU17—3E 28
Brookfield Rd. GU12—5E 20
Brook Gdns. GU14—4A 16
Brookhouse Rd. GU14—4J 15
Brooklands. GU11—7H 19
Brooklands Clo. GU9—2G 23
Brooklands Rd. GU9—2H 23
Brooklands Way. GU9—2H 23
Brookley Clo. GU10—6B 24
Brookly Gdns. GU13—5A 14
Brook Rd. GU15—2A 10
Brook Rd. GU19—3K 5
Brooksby Clo. GU17—1E 8
Brookside. GU9—3F 23

Brookside. GU17—6F 3
Brookwood Lye Rd. GU21
—7K 13
Brookwood Rd. GU14—3C 16
Broom Acres. GU13—5J 29
Broom Acres. GU17—5E 2
Broome Clo. GU17—2E 28
Broom Hill. GU10—1A 22
Broomhill Rd. GU14—2G 15
Broomleaf Corner. GU9—7G 23
Broomleaf Rd. GU9—7G 23
Broomrigg Rd. GU13—1G 29
Broomsquires Rd. GU19—3A 6
Broom Way. GU17—2H 9
Broomwood Way. GU10—4F 27
Brougham Pl. GU9—2E 22
Broughton M. GU16—5E 10
Browning Barracks. GU11
—3A 20
Browning Clo. GU15—2H 11
Brownsover Rd. GU14—3F 15
Browns Wlk. GU10—6C 26
Bruneval Barracks. GU11
—4J 19
Brunswick Dri. GU24—7E 12
Brunswick Rd. GU16 & GU24
—1H 17
Brunswick Rd. GU24—7C 12
Bruntile Clo. GU14—6C 16
Bryanstone Clo. GU13—2A 18
Bryn Rd. GU10—3C 26
Buchan, The. GU15—7F 5
Buckhurst Rd. GU16—1E 16
Buckingham Way. GU16
—5E 10
Buckland Clo. GU14—7B 10
Buller Barracks. GU11—4B 20
Buller Rd. GU11—4A 20
Bullers Rd. GU9—3H 23
Bullfinch Clo. GU15—5H 3
Buntings, The. GU9—2C 26
Bunyan's La. GU21—1K 13
Burdock Clo. GU18—5C 6
Burford Rd. GU15—2A 10
Burghead Clo. GU15—6G 3
Burgoyne Rd. GU15—7F 5
Burleigh Rd. GU16—6C 10
Burley Way. GU17—7F 3
Burlington Ct. GU11—7K 19
Burlington Ct. GU17—3G 9
Burne-Jones Dri. GU15—7F 5
Burnsall Clo. GU14—1A 16
Burns Av. GU13—2A 18
Burnside. GU13—2K 29
Burnt Hill Rd. GU10—4D 26
Burnt Hill Way. GU10—5E 26
Burnt Pollard La. GU18—4F 7
Burrell Rd. GU16—6B 10
Burrwood Gdns. GU12—4F 21
Burton Clo. GU20—1E 6
Busk Cres. GU14—4J 15
Butler Rd. GU19—3A 6
Buttermere Clo. GU14—3H 15
Buttermere Dri. GU15—1J 11
Byron Av. GU15—3G 11
Byron Clo. GU13—3K 29
Byron Clo. GU17—5D 28
Byron Dri. RG11—2E 2
Byways. GU17—4D 28
Byworth Clo. GU9—7C 22
Byworth Rd. GU9—7C 22

Cabrol Rd. GU14—2K 15
Cadet Way. GU13—4A 18
Cadnam Clo. GU11—3B 24
Cadogan Rd. GU16—1C 20
Caernarvon. GU16—6E 10
Caesar Ct. GU11—6H 19
Caesars Camp Rd. GU15—5F 5
Caesar's Clo. GU15—5E 4
Caesars Ct. GU9—3F 23
Cairn Clo. GU15—3G 11
Cairngorm Pl. GU14—7H 9
Caldwell Rd. GU20—1E 6
Calshot Way. GU16—7F 11

Calthorpe Rd. GU13—1H 29
Calvert Clo. GU12—7C 20
Calvin Clo. GU15—2G 11
Camberley Towers. GU15
—1C 10
(off Up. Gordon Rd.)
Cambrian Clo. GU15—1A 10
Cambrian Rd. GU14—7G 9
Cambridge Pl. GU9—7F 23
Cambridge Rd. GU11—6J 19
Cambridge Rd. GU15—4H 3
Cambridge Rd. RG11—1F 3
Cambridge Rd. E. GU14—6B 16
Cambridge Rd. W. GU14—6B 16
Cambridge Wlk. GU15—7B 4
Camden Wlk. GU13—6B 14
Cameron Rd. GU11—1C 20
Campbell Clo. GU13—2H 29
Campbell Clo. GU13—2H 29
Campbell Clo. GU17—7C 2
Campbell Rd. GU11—5K 19
Camp Farm Rd. GU11—3C 20
Campion Way. GU17—3J 9
Camp Rd. GU14—7B 16
Canada Rd. GU16—6J 11
Canal Bank. GU12—4F 21
Canal Cotts. GU12—4F 21
Canberra Clo. GU17—1D 28
Canning Rd. GU12—6C 20
Canterbury Rd. GU12—5F 21
Canterbury Rd. GU14—5C 16
Carfax Av. GU10—1E 24
Cargate Av. GU11—7K 19
Cargate Gro. GU11—7K 19
Cargate Hill. GU11—7J 19
Cargate Ter. GU11—7J 19
Carisbrooke. GU16—6E 10
Carlinwark Dri. GU15—6E 4
Carlton Clo. GU15—3G 11
Carlton Cres. GU13—2A 18
Carlyle Ct. RG11—1F 3
Carlyon Clo. GU14—3B 16
Carlyon Clo. GU16—3E 16
Carmarthen Clo. GU14—7K 9
Caroline Way. GU16—5E 10
Carrick La. GU17—7B 2
Carrington La. GU12—7F 17
Carshalton Rd. GU15—4F 5
Carthona Dri. GU13—4J 29
Cassino Clo. GU11—6A 20
Castle Clo. GU15—2G 3
Castlecraig Ct. GU15—6G 3
Castle Hill. GU9—6E 22
Castle Rd. GU11—4H 19
Castle Rd. GU15—2D 10
Castle St. GU9—6E 22
Castle St. GU13—4J 29
Castor Clo. GU13—3A 18
Castor Ct. GU17—2C 8
Caswell Ride. GU17—1C 8
Caswell Clo. GU14—1J 15
Catena Rise. GU18—4B 6
Catesby Gdns. GU17—4C 28
Cavalry Ct. GU11—6H 19
Cavan's Rd. GU11—2B 20
Cavendish Ct. GU17—3G 9
Cavendish M. GU15—7K 19
Cavendish Rd. GU11—7K 19
Cavendish Rd. GU13—7H 29
Caves Farm Clo. GU17—5D 2
Cedar Av. GU17—1G 9
Cedar Clo. GU12—1D 24
Cedar Clo. GU19—2K 5
Cedar Ct. GU11—6K 19
Cedar Dri. GU13—6B 14
Cedar Gro. GU24—2H 13
Cedar La. GU16—6C 10
Cedar Rd. GU14—4B 16
Cedars. GU17—5C 2
Cedars, The. GU13—7A 14
Cedarways. GU9—3E 26
Celandine Ct. GU17—2C 28
Celery La. GU10—5E 26
Cemetery Pales. GU24—7J 13
Cemetery Rd. GU13—4H 29
Centurion Clo. GU15—5G 3

Chaffinch Clo. GU15—5G 3
Chalfont Dri. GU14—5B 16
Chamber La. GU10—3A 26
Chambers Rd. GU12—3G 21
Chamomile Gdns. GU14—2F 15
Champion Way. GU13—6K 29
Chancery Gdns. GU10—4C 26
Chandlers La. GU17—2E 28
Chandlers Rd. GU12—4G 21
Chantreys. GU13—3G 29
Chantry Rd. GU19—3J 5
Chantrys, The. GU9—7C 22
Chapel Head. RG27—1A 28
Chapel La. GU14—6J 9
Chapel La. GU19—3J 5
Chapel La. GU10—6B 26
Chapel Rd. GU15—1A 10
Chapel St. GU14—1C 16
Chaplain's Hill. RG11—1G 3
Charlecote La. GU14—4D 16
Charlotte Clo. GU12—1G 23
Charlton Ct. GU15—4G 3
Chart House Rd. GU12—1F 21
Chartwell. GU16—1E 16
Chase, The. GU14—1C 16
Chatfield Clo. GU14—5B 16
Chatsworth Gro. GU9—3E 22
Chatsworth Heights.
—6F 5
Chatsworth La. GU14—4D 16
Chatton Row. GU24—4H 13
Chaucer Rd. GU14—1J 15
Chaucer Rd. RG11—1E 2
Chelwood Dri. GU17—4C 2
Chequers La. RG27—3A 28
Cherberry Clo. GU13—3A 14
Cheriton Way. GU17—1G 9
Cherrydale Rd. GU15—1J 11
Cherryhill Gro. GU11—7J 19
Cherry Tree Clo. GU9—6F 23
Cherry Tree La. GU14—2F 15
Cherry Tree Clo. GU15—4G 3
Cherry Tree Rd. GU10—7B 26
Cherry Tree Wlk. GU10—7B 26
(in two parts)
Cherrywood Rd. GU14—7K 9
Chertsey Rd. GU20 & GU24
—1E 6
Chesilton Cres. GU13—6K 29
Chester Clo. GU12—6G 21
Chester Rd. GU12—5G 21
Chesters Rd. GU15—1G 11
Chester Way. GU10—3E 24
Chestnut Av. GU9—2D 26
Chestnut Av. GU12—2D 24
Chestnut Av. GU15—7F 5
Chestnut Clo. GU13—3B 14
Chestnut Clo. GU17—4D 2
Chestnut Gro. GU13—5A 14
Chestnut La. GU24—1K 7
Chestnut Rd. GU14—2K 15
Cheswell Gdns. GU13—5H 29
Chetwode Pl. GU12—2B 24
Chetwode Ter. GU11—7H 19
Cheviot Clo. GU14—7H 9
Cheviot Clo. GU15—2H 11
Cheviot Dri. GU13—3A 14
Cheviot Rd. GU17—3C 2
Chewter Clo. GU19—2A 6
Cheylesmore Dri. GU16—3J 11
Cheyne Way. GU14—7J 9
Chichester Rd. GU12—5F 21
Chilham Clo. GU16—6E 10
Chillingham Way. GU15—2B 10
Chiltern Av. GU14—3G 15
Chiltern Clo. GU13—2A 18
Chiltern Clo. GU14—3G 15
Chiltern Clo. GU17—4C 2
Chine, The. GU10—5C 26
Chingford Av. GU14—2C 16
Chinnock Clo. GU13—4J 29
Chippendale Clo. GU17—3H 9
Chive Ct. GU14—3F 15
Chobham Rd. GU16—4D 10
Chobham Rd. GU21—4K 13
(Knaphill)
Chrismas Av. GU12—7B 20

Chrismas Pl. GU12—7B 20
Christchurch Clo. GU13—7J 29
Christchurch Dri. GU17—7F 3
Christie Clo. GU18—4D 6
Christie Wlk. GU17—5E 28
Christine Clo. GU12—7E 20
Church Av. GU14—3B 16
Church Circ. GU14—5B 16
Church Clo. GU24—7G 13
Church Ct. GU13—2H 29
(off Branksomewood Rd.)
Church Ct. GU13—2J 29
(off Church Rd.)
Church Gro. GU13—2H 29
Church Hill. GU12—1B 24
Church Hill. GU15—1D 10
Churchill Av. GU12—1B 24
Churchill Clo. GU14—6A 10
Churchill Cres. GU14—6A 10
Churchill Cres. GU17—1A 8
Church La. GU9—2H 23
Church La. GU10—7A 18
(Ewshot)
Church La. GU10—7B 26
(Rowledge)
Church La. GU12—6G 21
Church La. GU14—3H 15
Church La. GU21—2J 13
Church La. GU24—2H 13
(Bisley)
Church La. E. GU11—7K 19
Church La. W. GU11—7J 19
Church Pas. GU9—7E 22
Church Path. GU14—2F 21
Church Path. GU14—3B 16
(Farnborough Park)
Church Path. GU14—7B 16
(South Farnborough)
Church Path. GU14—3H 15
(West Heath)
Church Rd. GU11—2B 24
Church Rd. GU13—1H 29
Church Rd. GU14—4H 3
Church Rd. GU16—5C 10
Church Rd. GU17—4C 2
Church Rd. GU19—2J 5
Church Rd. GU20—1C 6
Church Rd. GU24—6G 7
Church Rd. RG11—1E 2
Church Rd. E. GU14—6C 16
Church Rd. W. GU14—6B 16
Church St. GU11—6J 19
Church St. RG11—1E 2
Church View. GU14—6F 21
Clandon Ct. GU14—4C 16
Clanfield Ride. GU17—1G 9
Clappers La. GU24—5K 7
Clare Mead. GU10—6C 26
Claremont Av. GU15—1E 10
Clarence Clo. GU12—6B 20
Clarence Rd. GU13—3J 29
Clarendon Ct. GU17—3G 9
Clarewood Dri. GU15—7D 4
Clarke Cres. GU15—6H 3
Clarks Hill. GU10—7A 22
Claycart Rd. GU11—4G 19
Claydon Gdns. GU17—5K 9
Clayton Rd. GU14—5J 9
Clearsprings. GU18—4B 6
Clevedon Clo. GU16—6F 11
Clevedon Ct. GU14—4C 16
Clewborough Dri. GU15—7G 5
Clews La. GU24—3H 13
Clifton Clo. GU10—6D 26
Clive Rd. GU12—7C 20
Clockhouse Rd. GU14—3A 16
Cloisters, The. GU16—5C 10
Close, The. GU9—1G 27
Close, The. GU15—5H 3
Close, The. GU16—6C 10
Close, The. GU18—4B 6
Closeworth Rd. GU14—7D 16
Clouston Rd. GU14—2J 15
Clover La. GU17—3C 28
Clubhouse Rd. GU11—3J 19
Club La. RG11—1G 3
Club Row. GU24—6E 12

Clumps Rd. GU10—6H 27
Coach Ho. Clo. GU16—3D 10
Cobbett's La. GU17—1C 8
Cobbetts Wlk. GU24—2H 13
Cobbetts Way. GU14—4C 26
Cochrane Pl. GU20—1E 6
Cock-A-Dobby. GU17—4D 2
Cody Rd. GU14—4J 15
Coe Clo. GU11—7K 19
Colenor Wood. GU10—4C 26
Colbeck. GU13—4A 18
Colbred Corner. GU13—3B 14
Cold Harbour La. GU14—6H 9
Coldharbour La. GU24—5G 7
Coleford Bri. Rd. GU16—3C 16
Coleford Clo. GU16—4E 16
Coleford Paddocks. GU16
—3E 16
Coleman Rd. GU12—7C 20
Coleridge Av. GU17—1B 8
Coleridge Clo. RG11—1F 3
Coleson Hill Rd. GU10—5C 26
Coleville Rd. GU12—2J 15
College Clo. GU15—5C 4
College Cres. GU15—5H 3
College Gdns. GU9—7E 22
College Ride. GU15—6C 4
College Ride. GU19—4F 5
College Rd. GU12—5F 21
College Rd. GU15—6H 3
Collier La. GU14—2G 15
Collingwood Grange Clo. GU14
—5G 5
Collingwood Rise. GU15—6F 5
Colne Way. GU12—7F 21
Colville Gdns. GU18—5D 6
Colwyn Clo. GU17—3E 28
Combe La. GU14—1K 15
Comfrey Clo. GU14—2F 15
Commercial Rd. GU12—1B 24
Commonfields. GU24—7G 7
Compton Clo. GU13—3A 18
Compton Clo. GU17—4F 3
Compton Rd. GU13—3A 18
Compton Way. GU10—7K 23
Conifer Clo. GU13—6J 29
Conifer Dri. GU15—7F 5
Coniston Clo. GU14—4H 15
Coniston Clo. GU15—2H 11
Coniston Ct. GU18—4C 6
Coniston Dri. GU9—3D 22
Coniston Way. GU13—6H 29
Connaught Barracks. GU11
—2C 20
Connaught Clo. GU17—3D 28
Connaught Clo. RG11—2C 2
Connaught Cres. GU24—7G 13
Connaught Rd. GU12—6B 20
Connaught Rd. GU13—3J 29
Connaught Rd. GU15—1E 10
Connaught Rd. GU19—2H 5
Connaught Rd. GU24—7G 13
Connop Way. GU16—3E 10
Constable Way. GU15—7H 3
Conway Clo. GU16—5E 10
Conway Rd. GU14—3G 15
Cookham Clo. GU17—4F 3
Coolarne Rise. GU16—7F 5
Coombe Clo. GU16—6C 10
Coombe Dri. GU13—6B 14
Coombe Rd. GU17—2D 28
Cooper Rd. GU20—6B 6
Cooper's Hill. RG27—6A 28
Coopers Hill Dri. GU24—7D 12
Coopers Ter. GU9—6F 23
Copelands Clo. GU15—2J 11
Copenhagen Wlk. RG11—1E 2
Copped Hall Dri. GU15—7H 5
Copped Hall Way. GU15—7H 5
Copperfield Av. GU15—3H 3
Coppice Clo. GU9—3H 23
Coppice Gdns. GU17—4E 28
Coppice Gdns. RG11—1C 2
Copse Av. GU9—2H 23
Copse Clo. GU15—7F 5
Copse End. GU13—3C 29
Copse End. GU15—7E 4

Copse La. GU13—6H 29
Copse La. RG27—1C 28
Copse, The. GU10—6C 26
Copse, The. GU14—4G 15
Copse Way. GU10—4C 26
Copthorne Dri. GU18—4C 6
Corbett Dri. GU18—6A 6
Cordwallies Rd. GU15—5E 4
Corfe Gdns. GU16—5E 10
Coriander Clo. GU14—3F 15
Cormorant Pl. GU15—6H 3
Cornbunting Clo. GU15—6G 3
Cornelia Clo. GU14—4G 15
Cornfield. GU17—5D 28
Cornwall Clo. GU15—6E 4
Coronation Rd. GU11—2A 24
Coronation Rd. GU17—6B 2
Corringway. GU13—2A 18
Cotswold Clo. GU14—7H 9
Cotswold Ct. GU13—2J 29
Cotswold Rd. GU17—4C 2
Cottage Gdns. GU14—3J 15
Cottrell Flats. GU14—7C 16
Cottrells Ct. GU13—7J 29
Courtenay Rd. GU9—2H 23
Court Gdns. GU15—1C 10
Courtmoor Av. GU13—4K 29
Court Rd. GU11—6K 19
Cove Rd. GU13—3A 14
Cove Rd. GU14—3J 15
Covert, The. GU14—6H 9
Covey Clo. GU14—6K 9
Cowshot Cres. GU24—7E 12
Cox Grn. GU15—7G 3
Coxheath Rd. GU13—5H 29
Coxmoor Clo. GU13—3B 18
Crabtree Rd. GU15—4A 10
Crake Pl. GU15—5G 3
Cranberry Wlk. GU17—3J 9
Cranbrook Ct. GU13—1K 29
Crane Ct. GU15—5G 3
Cranford Av. GU13—6H 29
Cranford Pk. Dri. GU17—7A 2
Cranleigh Ct. GU14—3J 15
Cranley Pl. GU21—5K 13
Cranmere Clo. GU11—7H 19
Cranmere Gdns. GU11—7G 19
Cranmere La. GU11—1G 23
Cranmore Rd. GU16—3F 17
Cranwell Gro. GU18—5A 6
Craven Clo. GU10—4F 27
Crawford Gdns. GU15—1A 10
Crawley Dri. GU15—7E 4
Crawley Hill. GU15—1E 10
Crawley Ridge. GU15—7E 4
Crawley Wood Clo. GU15
—1E 6
Credon Clo. GU14—2J 15
Cree's Meadow. GU20—2D 6
Crerar Clo. GU14—4G 15
Crescent Clo. GU12—3G 21
Crescent, The. GU9—3E 22
Crescent, The. GU13—5F 29
Crescent, The. GU14—4B 16
Crescent, The. GU17—2C 9
Cricketers La. GU20—1E 6
Cricket Field. RG11—1G 3
Cricket Field Gro. RG11—1G 3
Cricket Hill. GU17—3B 8
Cricket Hill La. GU17—3A 8
Cricket La. GU14—4G 27
Crimea Rd. GU11—6A 20
Cripley Rd. GU14—1G 15
Crofters Clo. GU17—5D 2
Croft La. GU17—2E 28
Croft Rd. GU11—1A 24
Croft, The. GU13—3G 29
Croft, The. GU17—6A 2
Croft Way. GU16—4E 10
Cromwell Rd. GU15—6C 4
Cromwell Way. GU14—7A 10
Crondal Ct. GU15—2A 10
Crondall End. GU17—2E 28
Crondall La. GU10—7A 22
Crondall Rd. GU13—6F 29
Crookham Rd. GU13—5H 29
Crooksbury Rd. GU10—6A 24

Crosby Gdns. GU17—2C 28
Crosby Hill Dri. GU15—6E 4
Cross Gdns. GU16—1E 16
Cross La. GU16—1E 16
Cross Rd. GU12—5G 21
Cross St. GU11—6K 19
Cross St. GU14—7B 16
Crossways. GU12—7B 20
Crossways. GU13—5F 29
Crown Dri. GU9—4K 23
Crown Gdns. GU13—7A 14
Crown La. GU9—4J 23
Crown Pl. GU15—4H 3
Crowthorne Rd. GU17—5D 2
Croyde Clo. GU14—1K 15
Cruikshank Lea. GU15—7H 3
Crundwell Ct. GU9—6G 23
Cuckoo La. GU17—7E 6
Cuckoo Vale. GU12—7E 6
Cullen Clo. GU17—4E 28
Culverlands Cres. GU12—5E 20
Culver Rd. GU15—6G 3
Cumberland Rd. GU15—1H 11
Cunnington Rd. GU14—5D 16
Curley Hill Rd. GU18—6K 5
Curtis Ct. GU13—6K 29
Curzon Dri. GU15—3A 18
Cuthbert Rd. GU12—2G 21
Cutts Rd. GU11—1C 20
Cygnet Ct. GU13—4A 14
Cypress Dri. GU13—6C 14
Cypress Gro. GU12—1E 20
Cypress Way. GU11—5A 4
Cyprus Rd. GU16—6J 11

Daffodil Dri. GU24—3H 13
Dale Clo. GU10—3C 26
Dale Gdns. GU17—5D 2
Dalston Clo. GU15—3J 11
Danebury Wlk. GU16—6E 10
Danesbury Wlk. GU16—6E 10
Darby Grn. La. GU17—1E 8
Darby Grn. Rd. GU17—1D 8
Dark La. GU20—1C 6
Darleydale Clo. GU15—3G 3
Darset Av. GU13—1K 29
Dart Rd. GU14—1G 15
Darvills La. GU9—7K 23
Darwin Gro. GU11—5B 20
Dawnay Rd. GU15—5A 4
Dawsmere Clo. GU15—1H 11
Deadbrook La. GU11 & GU12
—4D 20
Dead End. GU14—1J 19
Dean Pde. GU15—5E 4
Deans Ct. GU20—2E 6
Deedman Clo. GU12—6F 21
Deepcut Bri. Rd. GU16—1H 17
Deepdene. GU10—4G 27
Deep Well Dri. GU15—1D 10
Deer Rock Rd. GU15—6E 4
Dell Gro. GU16—4E 10
Dell, The. GU9—2G 23
Dell, The. GU17—4E 28
Delville Ct. GU14—4G 15
Dene Clo. GU14—4H 27
Dene La. GU10—4G 27
Dene La. W. GU10—5H 27
Dene Rd. GU14—4J 15
Dene Wlk. GU10—4G 27
Denham Clo. GU13—6B 14
Denham Dri. GU17—1A 8
Denly Way. GU18—4D 6
Denmark Sq. GU12—6C 20
Denmark St. GU12—6C 20
Denning Clo. GU13—4H 29
Dennistoun Clo. GU15—1C 10
Denton Way. GU16—4C 10
Derek Horn Ct. GU15—7A 4
Derry Rd. GU14—6J 9
Derwent Av. GU14—4E 20
Derwent Clo. GU14—3H 15
Derwent Dri. GU9—3D 22
Derwent Rd. GU18—5C 6
Dettingen Barracks. GU16
—5J 11

Dettingen Rd. GU16—6K 11
Devils Highway, The. RG11
—1B 2
Devon Clo. GU13—3A 14
Devon Clo. GU15—6G 3
Devonshire Dri. GU15—6E 4
Dexter Way. GU13—3A 14
Diamond Hill. GU15—6D 4
Diamond Ridge. GU15—6C 4
Dickens Way. GU17—4E 28
Dinorben Av. GU13—4H 29
Dinorben Beeches. GU13
—4H 29
Dinorben Clo. GU13—4H 29
Dippenhall Rd. GU10—7A 22
Dogflud Way. GU9—6F 23
Dollis Dri. GU9—6G 23
Domen Rd. GU15—2J 9
Donnington Clo. GU15—2A 10
Dora's Grn. La. GU10—2A 22
Doreen Clo. GU14—7H 9
Dorking Vs. GU21—4K 13
Dormer Clo. RG11—1D 2
Dorset Rd. GU12—3G 21
Douai Clo. GU14—3B 16
Douglas Gro. GU10—5F 27
Dovedale Clo. GU15—3G 3
Downing St. GU9—7E 22
Doyle Gdns. GU17—5E 28
Dragoon Ct. GU11—6H 19
Drake Av. GU14—6F 17
Drayhorse Dri. GU15—3K 5
Drovers End. GU13—3B 14
Drovers Way. GU9—3D 22
Drovers Way. GU13—3B 14
Dryden Rd. GU14—1J 15
Duchess of Kent Barracks. GU11
—5A 20
Dudley Ct. GU13—5K 29
Duke of Connaught's Rd. GU11
—1B 20
Duke of Cornwall Av. GU15
—4C 4
Dukes Clo. GU9—3D 22
Dukes Mead. GU13—2G 29
Duke's Ride. RG11—1B 2
Duke's Ter. GU11—5A 20
Dukes Wlk. GU9—3D 22
Dumas Clo. GU17—4E 28
Dunbar Rd. GU16—7E 10
Dundaff Clo. GU15—1F 11
Dungells Farm Clo. GU17—2A 8
Dungells La. GU17—5E 28
Dunmow Hill. GU13—1K 29.
Dunsmore Gdns. GU17—4C 28
Durham Rd. GU15—3H 3
Durnsford Av. GU13—4K 29
Duval Pl. GU19—2K 5

Eagles Nest. GU17—4D 2
Earlsbourne. GU13—4A 18
Earls Gro. GU15—7D 4
East Av. GU9—3G 23
Eastern La. RG11—1H 3
Eastern Rd. GU12—6C 20
East Grn. GU17—2F 9
Eastmead. GU14—3A 16
E. Ring. GU10—2F 25
E. Station Rd. GU12—7A 20
East St. GU9—6F 23
Eaton Rd. GU15—2A 10
Echo Barn La. GU10—5B 26
Eddy Rd. GU12—7B 20
Edgbarrow Rise. GU17—3D 2
Edgcumbe Pk. Dri. RG11—1D 2
Edgedale Clo. RG11—1E 2
Edgemoor Rd. GU16—3H 11
Edinburgh Clo. GU12—3F 21
Edney Clo. GU13—2A 18
Edward Av. GU15—1K 9
Edward Rd. GU9—3F 27
Edward Rd. GU20—1E 6
Edward St. GU11—6J 19
Eelmoor Plain Rd. GU11—4G 19
Eelmoor Rd. GU11—3G 19
Eelmoor Rd. GU14—5J 15

Egerton Rd. GU15—7J 3
Eggar's Hill. GU11—1K 23
Eland Rd. GU12—7C 20
Elcho Rd. GU24—6D 12
Elder Rd. GU24—2H 13
Eldon Dri. GU10—5G 27
Elgin Way. GU16—6E 10
Elizabeth Av. GU19—3A 6
Elizabeth Dri. GU13—6K 29
Elleray Ct. GU12—3F 21
Elles Rd. GU14—5H 15
Ellison Way. GU10—2E 24
Elm Bank. GU17—2E 28
Elm Ct. GU15—5K 19
Elm Cres. GU9—2G 23
Elmcroft Clo. GU16—7E 10
Elm Gro. GU9—2F 23
Elm Gro. GU24—3H 13
Elmgrove Rd. GU14—3A 16
Elm La. GU10—1E 24
Elm Pl. GU11—1B 24
Elm Rd. GU9—2G 23
Elmsleigh Rd. GU14—3J 15
Elms Rd. GU11—7K 19
Elms Rd. GU13—6B 14
Elms, The. GU10—1E 24
Elms, The. GU17—2G 9
Elm View. GU12—5G 21
Elsenwood Cres. GU15—6F 5
Elsenwood Dri. GU15—6F 5
Elsley Clo. GU16—1E 16
Elstead Rd. GU10—4F 25
Elston Pl. GU12—1B 24
Elston Rd. GU12—1B 24
Elvetham Clo. GU13—1K 29
Elvetham Pl. GU13—1H 29
Elvetham Rd. GU13—1G 29
Ely Clo. GU16—7F 11
Empress Av. GU14—2A 16
Enfield Rd. GU12—3G 21
Englesfield. GU15—1H 11
Ennerdale Gro. GU9—3D 22
Epsom Clo. GU15—5B 4
Ernest Ter. Clo. GU10—4E 26
Esher Rd. GU15—4F 5
Eskdale Way. GU15—2J 11
Essex Clo. GU16—7F 11
Eton Pl. GU9—2E 22
Evelyn Av. GU11—1A 24
Evelyn Wood's Rd. GU11
—1B 20
Evenlode Way. GU17—5F 3
Everest Rd. GU15—5C 4
Evergreen Rd. GU16—4E 10
Eversley Rd. GU17—2C 28
Evesham Wlk. GU15—4G 3
Ewins Clo. GU12—6F 21
Ewshot La. GU13—7J 29
Exeter Gdns. GU17—2D 28
Exeter Rd. GU12—5F 21

Fairacres. GU10—6C 26
Fairfax Rd. GU14—7A 10
Fairfield Clo. GU16—4H 9
Fairfield La. GU24—6H 7
Fairfield, The. GU9—7F 23
(in two parts)
Fairholme. GU9—1F 27
Fairland Clo. GU13—7A 14
Fairmead Clo. GU15—6H 3
Fairmile. GU13—5J 29
Fair View Gdns. GU9—3G 23
Fairview Rd. GU12—5G 21
Fairway Heights. GU15—7G 5
Fairway, The. GU9—2G 23
Fairway, The. GU14—7E 14
Fairway, The. GU15—3F 11
Fakenham Way. GU15—4G 3
Falaise Clo. GU11—6A 20
Falcon Clo. GU16—5C 10
Falcon Way. GU17—3D 28
Falkner Rd. GU9—7E 22
Falkners Clo. GU13—3B 14
Fallowfield. GU13—3B 14
Fallowfield. GU17—2D 28
Falmouth Clo. GU15—2F 11

Faraday Rd. GU14—1B 16
Farcrosse Clo. GU17—5F 3
Fareham Dri. GU17—2D 28
Faringdon Clo. GU17—4F 3
Farm Clo. GU17—1A 8
Farm Dri. GU13—3A 14
Farm Rd. GU12—5D 20
Farm Rd. GU16—4D 10
Farm View. GU17—1A 8
Farm Wlk. GU12—1H 25
Farnborough Aerospace &
Business Pk. GU14—7K 15
Farnborough Business Pk. GU14
—5K 15
Farnborough Rd. GU9, GU11 &
GU14—1G 23
Farnborough St. GU14—1C 16
Farnham Business Centre. GU9
—6G 23
Farnham By-Pass. GU9—2C 26
Farnham Pk. Clo. GU9—3E 22
Farnham Pk. Dri. GU9—3E 22
Farnham Rd. GU10—2A 22
(Ewshot)
Farnham Rd. GU10—7A 26
(Holt Pound)
Farnham Rd. GU13—7C 14
Farnham Trading Est. GU9
—5J 23
Farrell Clo. GU15—3B 10
Faulkner Pl. GU15—1K 5
Faversham Rd. GU15—4G 3
Felbridge Clo. GU16—4E 10
Fellow Grn. GU24—7G 7
Fellow Grn. Rd. GU24—7G 7
Fellows Rd. GU14—6C 16
Fennel Clo. GU14—3E 14
Fenns La. GU24—7F 7
Fenn's Yd. GU9—7E 22
Ferbies. GU13—5K 29
Fernbrae Clo. GU10—7E 26
Fern Clo. GU16—3H 11
Fern Ct. GU12—7E 20
Ferndale Rd. GU13—7J 29
Fern Dri. GU13—5H 29
Fernhill Clo. GU9—3E 22
Fernhill Clo. GU13—5J 9
Fernhill Dri. GU9—3E 22
Fernhill La. GU9—3E 22
Fernhill La. GU17—5H 9
Fernhill Rd. GU17 & GU14
—4H 9
Fernhill Wlk. GU17—5J 9
Ferniehurst. GU15—2E 10
Fernleigh Rise. GU16—7H 11
Ferns, The. GU9—2F 23
Field End. GU9—5J 23
Field End. GU24—7G 7
Fieldfare Av. GU17—3D 28
Fielding Gdns. RG11—1E 2
Fielding Rd. GU14—7H 3
Field La. GU16—5C 10
Field Path. GU14—5J 9
Field Rd. GU14—5J 9
Field Stores App. GU11—5B 20
Field Way. GU10—2E 24
Field Way. GU12—5D 20
Fieldway. GU13—3G 29
Fincham End Dri. RG11—1C 2
Finch Clo. GU21—4K 13
Findhorn Clo. GU15—6G 3
Findings, The. GU14—6H 9
Finney Dri. GU20—1E 6
Fintry Pl. GU14—7H 9
Fintry Wlk. GU14—7H 9
Fir Acre Rd. GU12—2E 20
Fir Clo. GU13—3J 29
Fircroft. GU13—2J 29
Fir Dri. GU17—3G 9
Firethorn Clo. GU13—4K 29
Firfield Rd. GU9—3D 26
Firglen Dri. GU17—6A 2
Firgrove Ct. GU9—1F 27
Firgrove Clo. GU14—3A 16
Firgrove Hill. GU9—1F 27
Firgrove Pde. GU14—3A 16
Firgrove Rd. GU14—3A 16

Firgrove Rd. RG27 & GU17
—3B 28
Firlands Av. GU15—1C 10
Firs Clo. GU14—5B 16
Firs, The. GU24—3H 13
Fir Tree All. GU11—6K 19
Firtree Clo. GU17—4C 2
Fir Tree Way. GU13—7A 14
Firwood Dri. GU15—1B 10
Fitzroy Rd. GU13—1G 29
Flats, The. GU17—2E 8
Fleet Rd. GU13 & GU14—4C 14
(Farnborough)
Fleet Rd. GU13—2J 29
(Fleet)
Fleet Rd. GU14 & GU11—1D 18
Fleet Rd. RG27—1F 29
Fleming Clo. GU14—1C 16
Flexlands La. GU13—2A 18
Florence Clo. GU17—3E 28
Florence Rd. GU13—2A 18
Florence Rd. GU15—6G 3
Folly Clo. GU13—4K 29
Follyhatch La. GU12—5H 21
Folly Hill. GU9—3D 22
Folly La. N. GU9—2E 22
Folly La. S. GU9—3D 22
Forbes Chase. GU15—6G 3
Ford La. GU10—4E 26
Ford Rd. GU24—1F 13
(Bisley)
Ford Rd. GU24—4K 7
(Chobham)
Foreman Pk. GU12—6G 21
Foreman Rd. GU12—7G 21
Forest Dean. GU13—3B 14
Forest Dri. GU10—6F 27
Forest End. GU13—5J 29
Forest End. GU17—4C 2
Forest End Rd. GU17—4C 2
Forest Glade. GU10—7A 26
Forest Hills. GU15—2A 10
Forge Clo. GU9—6G 23
Forge La. GU11—2J 19
Forth Clo. GU14—1G 15
Fort Narrien. GU15—7H 3
Fortrose Clo. GU15—1B 10
Fosseway. RG11—1C 2
Fossewood Dri. GU15—5C 4
Fosters La. GU21—4K 13
Fowler Rd. GU14—1J 15
Fowler's Rd. GU11—2C 20
Fox Covert. GU18—5B 6
Foxcroft. GU13—6K 29
Foxdown Clo. GU15—1B 10
Fox Dri. GU17—6A 2
Foxhill Cres. GU15—5G 5
Fox Hills La. GU12—7A 20
Foxhurst Rd. GU12—3F 21
Fox La. RG27—1B 28
Foxley Clo. GU17—1F 9
Fox Rd. GU10—3F 27
Fox Way. GU10—2A 22
Foxwood. GU13—4B 14
Fox Yd. GU9—7E 22
Foye La. GU13—3A 18
France Hill Dri. GU15—1B 10
Fraser Mead. GU15—7H 3
Frederick St. GU11—6K 19
Freelands Dri. GU13—6H 29
Freemantle Clo. GU19—1K 5
Freemantle Rd. GU19—2A 6
Freesia Rd. GU24—3H 13
French Gdns. GU17—2G 9
Frensham Av. GU13—6B 14
Frensham Clo. GU17—3D 28
Frensham Heights Rd. GU10
—7D 26
Frensham Rd. GU9 & GU10
—2F 27
Frensham Vale. GU10—6E 26
Frere Av. GU13—4H 29
Freshwood Dri. GU17—2A 8
Friend Av. GU12—7C 20
Friesian Clo. GU13—3A 14
Frimley Business Pk. GU16
—6B 10

Frimley By-Pass. GU16—6B 10
Frimley Grn. Rd. GU16—6D 10
Frimley Gro. Gdns. GU16
—5C 10
Frimley Hall Dri. GU15—7E 4
Frimley High St. GU16—5C 10
Frimley Rd. GU12—6F 17
Frimley Rd. GU15—1K 9
Frith Hill Rd. GU16—5F 11
Frodsham Way. GU15—3H 3
Frogmore Ct. GU17—2F 9
Frogmore Gro. GU17—2F 9
Frogmore Pk. Dri. GU17—2F 9
Frogmore Rd. GU17—1E 8
Frome Clo. GU14—1G 15
Fromow Gdns. GU20—1E 6
Fry's Acre. GU12—5F 21
Fry's La. GU17—6B 2
Fugelmere Rd. GU13—5B 14
Fugelmere Wlk. GU13—5B 14
(in two parts)
Fullers Rd. GU10—6A 26
Furze Hill. GU10—6C 24
Furze Hill Cres. RG11—1F 3
Fyfield Clo. GU17—1G 9

Gables Clo. GU12—3F 21
Gables Clo. GU14—3K 15
Gables Rd. GU13—7J 29
Gaffney Clo. GU11—1C 20
Gainsborough Clo. GU14
—5C 16
Gainsborough Clo. GU15—6E 4
Gainsborough Ct. GU13—2K 29
Gale Dri. GU18—4B 6
Gallery Rd. GU24—6E 12
Gallop, The. GU17—6A 2
Galloway Clo. GU13—3B 14
Gallwey Rd. GU11—5A 20
Gally Hill Rd. GU13—6H 29
Gapemouth Rd. GU24—2J 17
Garbetts Way. GU10—3E 24
Gardener's Hill Rd. GU10
—5E 26
Gardens, The. GU10—2E 24
Garfield Rd. GU15—1B 10
Garnet Field. GU17—4C 28
Garrick Way. GU16—7F 11
Garth Clo. GU9—3D 26
Garth, The. GU12—7E 20
Garth, The. GU14—3C 16
Georgeham Rd. GU15—3G 3
George Rd. GU13—6A 14
George St. GU24—7B 12
Georgian Clo. GU15—6D 4
Georgina Ct. GU13—2K 29
Germander Dri. GU24—2H 13
Gibbet La. GU15—5F 5
Gibbons Clo. GU17—5F 3
Gibbs Way. GU17—5D 28
Gibraltar Barracks. GU17
—4B 8
Giffard Dri. GU14—2J 15
Giffards Meadow. GU9—1H 27
Gilbert Rd. GU15—5B 10
Gillian Av. GU12—1B 24
Gillian Clo. GU12—1C 24
Girton Clo. GU15—4H 3
Glamis Clo. GU16—7E 10
Glassonby Wlk. GU15—1H 11
Glebe Clo. GU10—4D 6
Glebe Ct. GU13—2J 29
Glebeland Rd. GU15—2J 9
Glebe Rd. GU14—2J 15
Glebe, The. GU17—2H 9
Glenavon Gdns. GU17—2A 8
Glencoe Clo. GU16—6F 11
Glendale Pk. GU13—1G 29
Gleneagles Clo. GU14—4F 15
Glenhurst Clo. GU17—2H 9
Glenmore Clo. GU12—2H 21
Glennines. GU15—4J 3
Glenmount Rd. GU16—5F 17
Glen Rd. GU15—2J 9
Globe Farm La. GU17—1E 8
Glorney Mead. GU9—3K 23
Gloucester Clo. GU16—1D 16

Gloucester Gdns. GU19—2K 5
Gloucester Rd. GU11—2B 24
Gloucester Rd. GU19—2K 5
Glynswood. GU10—6D 26
Glynswood. GU15—3E 10
Goddards La. GU15—3A 10
Goldcrest Clo. GU17—3D 28
Gold Hill. GU10—4F 27
Goldney Rd. GU15—2G 11
Goldsmith Way. RG11—1E 2
Golf Dri. GU15—2E 10
Gong Hill. GU10—7G 27
Gong Hill Dri. GU10—6G 27
Gooden Cres. GU14—4J 15
Goodwood Clo. GU15—5B 4
Goodwood Pl. GU14—4D 16
Gordon Av. GU13—2A 18
Gordon Av. GU15—2A 10
Gordon Cres. GU15—2B 10
Gordon Rd. GU11—7K 19
Gordon Rd. GU15—7C 16
Gordon Rd. GU15—2B 10
Gordon Rd. RG11—2G 3
Gordon Wlk. GU17—1B 8
Gorse Clo. GU10—4D 26
Gorseland. GU17—5E 28
Gorselands. GU9—2F 23
Gorselands Clo. GU12—3F 21
Gorse La. GU10—4E 26
Gorse Path. GU10—4D 26
Gorse Rd. GU16—4D 10
Gorse Way. GU13—4K 29
Gort Clo. GU11—1D 20
Gosden Rd. GU14—7G 7
Gosnell Clo. GU16—3J 11
Gough Rd. GU13—1H 29
Gough's Meadow. GU17—6E 2
Government Ho. Rd. GU11
—1K 19
Government Rd. GU11—4C 20
Governor's Rd. GU15—7J 3
Gower Pk. GU15—6G 3
Grace Bennett Clo. GU14—7K 9
Grace Reynolds Wlk. GU15
—7C 4
Graham Rd. GU20—1D 6
Grampian Rd. GU17—3D 2
Grand Av. GU15—7B 4
Grange Farm Rd. GU12—5F 21
Grange Rd. GU10—4C 24
(Tongham)
Grange Rd. GU12—6G 21
Grange Rd. GU13—6J 29
Grange Rd. GU14—7A 10
Grange Rd. GU15—1D 10
Grantham Clo. GU15—4H 3
Grantley Ct. GU9—4C 26
Grantley Dri. GU13—4J 29
Grant Rd. RG11—2F 3
Grasmere Way. GU9—3D 22
Grasmere Rd. GU14—4H 15
Grasmere Rd. GU18—4C 6
Gravel Rd. GU9—2E 22
Gravel Rd. GU13—2A 18
Gravel Rd. GU14—7C 16
Grayshott Dri. GU17—1F 9
Grayswood Dri. GU16—6F 17
Gt. Austins. GU14—6K 9
Greatfield Rd. GU14—6K 9
Green Acre. GU11—7J 19
Greenbank Way. GU15—4C 10
Greencroft. GU14—3A 16
Green Farm Rd. GU19—2A 6
Greenfield. GU9—3D 26
Greenfield Rd. GU9—3C 26
Greenhaven. GU17—4D 28
Greenhill Clo. GU9—3D 26
Greenhill Clo. GU15—7H 5
Greenhill Rd. GU9—3G 27
Green Hill Rd. GU15—7H 5
Greenhill Way. GU9—4D 26
Greenholme. GU15—1J 11
Greenlands Clo. GU15—5A 10
Green La. GU9—2D 26
(Farnham)

Green La. GU9—3J 23
(Weybourne)
Green La. GU17—2H 9
(Blackwater)
Green La. GU17—2E 8
(Frogmore)
Green La. GU17—6F 3
(Sandhurst)
Green La. GU17—3D 28
(Yateley)
Green La. GU19—3A 6
Green La. Cotts. GU9—4J 23
Green La. E. GU3—1K 25
Green La. W. GU12—1K 25
Greenleas. GU16—4D 10
Greenleas Clo. GU17—2E 28
Green Leys. GU13—7J 29
Green, The. GU9—4K 23
(Badshot Lea)
Green, The. GU9—3F 23
(Farnham)
Green, The. GU10—7D 24
Green, The. GU16—1E 16
Green, The. GU17—2F 9
(Blackwater)
Green, The. GU17—3D 28
(Yateley)
Green Way. GU12—5D 20
Greenways. GU13—5J 29
Greenways. GU17—4E 2
Greenwood Rd. GU24—7C 12
Grenadier Rd. GU12—4G 21
Grenadiers Way. GU14—4F 15
Grenville Dri. GU13—5H 29
Grenville Gdns. GU16—1D 16
Gresham Way. GU16—1D 16
Greyfriars Dri. GU24—2H 13
Greyhound Clo. GU12—7E 20
Greys Clo. GU11—6H 19
Greystead Pk. GU10—5B 26
Greystoke Ct. RG11—1D 2
Grieve Clo. GU10—2D 24
Griffon Clo. GU14—5J 15
Grindstone Cres. GU21—5J 13
Grosvenor Ct. GU17—3G 9
Grosvenor Rd. GU11—6K 19
Grove Cross Rd. GU16—5C 10
Grove Clo. GU19—1A 6
Grove End Rd. GU9—3E 26
Grovefields Av. GU17—5C 10
Grovelands. GU10—3H 27
Grove Rd. GU12—4F 21
Grove Rd. GU13—3A 18
Grove Rd. GU15—1E 10
Grove, The. GU11—7K 19
Grove, The. GU14—6C 16
Grove, The. GU15—5C 10
Guernsey Dri. GU13—3A 14
Guildford Rd. GU9 & GU10
—6G 23
Guildford Rd. GU12—2C 24
(Aldershot)
Guildford Rd. GU12 & GU3
—5H 21
(Ash)
Guildford Rd. GU13—7B 14
Guildford Rd. GU16—1E 16
Guildford Rd. GU19—2K 5
(in two parts)
Guildford Rd. E. GU14—6B 16
Guildford Rd. Trading Est. GU9
—6H 23
Guildford Rd. W. GU14—6B 16
Guillemont Fields. GU14
—2G 15
Gun Hill. GU11—5A 20

Habershon Dri. GU16—4J 11
Hadleigh Gdns. GU16—1D 16
Hadrians. GU9—5H 23
Hagley Rd. GU13—1H 29
Haig La. GU13—3A 18
Haig Rd. GU12—7B 20
Haig Rd. GU15—7J 3
Hailsham Clo. GU15—4G 3

Halebourne La. GU24—2H 7
Hale Reeds. GU9—3G 23
Hale Rd. GU9—4G 23
Hale Way. GU16—6C 10
Half Moon St. GU9—2K 5
Halimote Rd. GU11—7K 19
Hall Clo. GU15—7D 4
Hall Farm Cres. GU17—1A 8
Hall La. GU17—1E 28
Hamble Av. GU17—1G 9
Hambleton Clo. GU16—3G 11
Hamesmoor Rd. GU16—3D 16
Hamesmoor Way. GU16—3E 16
Hamilton Rd. GU13—2A 18
Hammersley Rd. GU11—1A 20
Hammond Way. GU18—4C 6
Hampshire Clo. GU12—2C 24
Hampshire Rd. GU15—5E 4
Hampton Clo. GU13—7K 29
Hampton Rd. GU9—3D 22
Hancombe Rd. GU17—4D 2
Handford La. GU17—1A 8
Hangerfield Clo. GU17—4E 28
Hanover Clo. GU16—5D 10
Hanover Clo. GU17—6A 2
Hanover Dri. GU13—3B 14
Hanover Gdns. GU14—1H 15
Harbour Clo. GU14—6K 9
Harcourt Rd. GU15—1A 10
Hardy Av. GU17—5E 28
Harlech Rd. GU17—2G 9
Harlington Way. GU13—2J 29
Harper's Rd. GU12—5H 21
Harpton Clo. GU17—6A 2
Harpton Pde. GU17—6A 2
Hart Centre, The. GU13—2J 29
Hartford Rise. GU15—7C 4
Hartland Pl. GU14—1K 15
Hartley Clo. GU17—1E 8
Hart Rd. GU14—1K 19
Hartsleaf Clo. GU13—3J 29
Harts Leap Clo. GU17—4E 2
Harts Leap Rd. GU17—5D 2
Harts Yd. GU9—7E 22
Hart, The. GU9—7E 22
Harvard Rd. GU15—4H 3
Harvest Clo. GU17—5D 28
Harvest Cres. GU13—2A 14
Harvey Rd. GU14—2F 15
Haslemere Clo. GU16—3H 11
Hastings Clo. GU16—7F 11
Hatch End. GU20—1D 6
Hatches, The. GU9—2D 26
Hatches, The. GU16—1C 16
Hatfield Gdns. GU14—4D 16
Hatherwood. GU17—1C 8
Hatton Hill. GU20—1D 6
Haven Way. GU9—5G 23
Hawkesworth Dri. GU19—4J 5
Hawkins Gro. GU13—5G 29
Hawkins Way. GU13—7B 14
Hawkswood Av. GU16—4E 10
Hawkwell. GU13—4A 18
Hawley Ct. GU14—6H 9
Hawley Grn. GU17—3H 9
Hawley La. GU17 & GU14—5K 9
Hawley Rd. GU17—2G 9
Hawthorn Clo. GU12—1D 24
Hawthorn Cotts. GU10—4A 24
Hawthorne Cres. GU17—2H 9
Hawthorn La. GU17—2H 9
Hawthorn Rd. GU16—4E 10
Hawthorn Way. GU24—3H 13
Haywood Dri. GU13—4K 29
Hazel Av. GU14—5J 15
Hazell Rd. GU9—7C 22
Hazel Rd. GU12—2H 25
Hazel Rd. GU16—5F 17
H. Jones Cres. GU11—5B 20
Hearmon Clo. GU17—7B 2
Hearsey Gdns. GU17—7E 2
(in two parts)
Heath Clo. GU9—2F 23
Heathcote Rd. GU12—5G 21
Heathcote Rd. GU15—1C 10
Heath Cotts. GU10—7G 27

Heath Dri. GU14—7H 13
Heather Clo. GU9—4C 26
Heather Clo. GU11—7H 19
Heather Clo. GU12—3G 21
Heatherdale Rd. GU15—2B 10
Heatherdene Av. RG11—1B 2
Heather Dri. GU13—6J 29
Heatherley Clo. GU15—1A 10
Heatherley Rd. GU15—1A 10
Heather Mead. GU16—4E 10
Heather Mead Ct. GU16—4E 10
Heather Ridge Arc. GU15
—2H 11
Heather Wlk. GU24—7E 12
Heathfield Clo. GU13—4H 29
Heath Hill Rd. RG11—1E 2
Heathlands Ct. GU17—2B 8
Heathland St. GU11—6K 19
Heath La. GU9—2F 23
Heath La. GU10—2A 22
Heathpark Dri. GU20—1F 7
Heath Ride. RG11—1A 2
Heath Rise. GU15—1C 10
Heath Rd. GU19—2K 5
Heathvale Bri. Rd. GU12—2F 21
Heathway. GU15—1C 10
Heathway Clo. GU15—1C 10
Heathwood Clo. GU17—6A 2
Heathyfields Rd. GU9—3C 22
Heddon Wlk. GU14—7H 13
Hedge Croft. GU17—3D 28
Heenan Clo. GU16—7D 10
Helen Ct. GU14—3A 16
Helston Clo. GU16—7F 11
Henley Clo. GU14—6H 9
Henley Dri. GU16—7D 10
Henley Gdns. GU17—1A 8
Herbert Rd. GU13—2H 29
Hereford La. GU9—3E 22
Hereford Mead. GU13—3A 14
Hermes Clo. GU13—6B 14
Hermitage Clo. GU14—6C 16
Hermitage Clo. GU16—5E 10
Hermitage Rd. GU21—7K 13
Heron Clo. GU13—2B 18
Heron Clo. GU16—3E 16
Herons Ct. GU18—5D 6
Herons Way. GU24—7E 12
Heron Wood Rd. GU12—1C 24
Herrett St. GU12—1C 24
Herrick Clo. GU16—3H 11
Herrings La. GU20—1E 6
Herriot Clo. GU17—5E 28
Hewlett Pl. GU19—2A 6
Hexham Clo. GU15—3G 3
Hicks La. GU17—1E 8
Higgs La. GU19—2J 5
Highams La. GU24—1H 7
High Beeches. GU16—4J 5
Highbury Cres. GU15—6F 5
Highclere Ct. GU21—4K 13
Highclere Dri. GU15—6F 5
Highclere Gdns. GU21—4K 13
Highclere Rd. GU12—1C 24
Highclere Rd. GU21—4K 13
High Copse. GU9—3D 22
Highdown. GU13—1K 29
Highfield Av. GU11—2K 23
Highfield Clo. GU9—3E 26
Highfield Clo. GU11—1A 24
Highfield Clo. GU14—3J 15
Highfield Gdns. GU11—1K 23
Highfield Path. GU14—3J 15
Highfield Rd. GU14—3J 15
Highgate La. GU14—3B 16
Highland Dri. GU13—3B 14
Highland Rd. GU12—6C 20
Highland Rd. GU15—5D 4
Highlands Clo. GU9—3E 26
Highlands Rd. GU9—2F 23
High Pk. Rd. GU9—6E 22
High St. Aldershot, GU11 & GU12
—6K 19
High St. Bagshot, GU19—2K 5
High St. Camberley, GU15
—7C 4

High St. Crowthorne, RG11
—1F 3
High St. Farnborough, GU14
—7C 16
High St. Knaphill, GU21—4K 13
High St. Little Sandhurst, GU17
—4C 2
High St. Rowledge, GU10
—7B 26
High St. Sandhurst, GU17
—4C 2
High St. West End, GU24—6G 7
High View Clo. GU14—3K 15
Highview Cres. GU15—4E 4
High View Rd. GU14—3K 15
High View Rd. GU18—5K 5
Highwood Clo. GU17—2A 8
Hilder Gdns. GU14—4C 16
Hilfield. GU17—1C 8
Hillary Clo. GU9—2E 26
Hillary Rd. GU9—3E 26
Hillbrook Rise. GU9—3E 22
Hillcrest. GU13—1K 29
Hill Crest Dri. GU9—4C 26
Hillcrest Rd. GU15—6C 5
Hill Rd. GU9—2G 23
Hillsborough Pk. GU15—1H 11
Hillside. GU15—6J 3
Hillside Clo. GU13—5F 29
Hillside Cres. GU16—7E 10
Hillside La. GU9—1G 23
Hillside Rd. GU9—2H 23
Hillside Rd. GU10—7F 27
Hillside Rd. GU11—1J 23
Hillside Rd. GU12—5G 21
Hilltop View. GU17—4D 28
Hill View Rd. GU9—7C 22
Hindell Clo. GU14—6K 9
Hinstock Clo. GU14—4K 15
Hitches La. GU13—5F 29
Hodges Clo. GU19—4J 5
Hogarth Clo. GU15—7H 3
Hoghatch La. GU9—3D 22
Hog's Back. GU10, GU3 & GU2
—5C 24
Holbeche Clo. GU14—4C 28
Holbrook Clo. GU9—1J 23
Holbrook Way. GU11—2A 24
Holder Rd. GU12—7D 20
Holland Clo. GU9—2H 27
Holland Gdns. GU13—3K 29
Hollis Wood Dri. GU10—5B 26
Holly Av. GU16—3G 11
Hollybank. GU24—7G 7
Hollybush La. GU17—2A 10
Hollybush La. RG27—1A 28
Holly Clo. GU12—6B 20
Holly Clo. GU14—3K 15
Holly Clo. RG27—2A 28
Holly Hedge Clo. GU16—4D 10
Holly Hedge Rd. GU16—4D 10
Hollyhock Dri. GU24—2H 13
Holly Rd. GU12—6B 20
Holly Rd. GU14—3J 15
Hollytree Gdns. GU16—6C 10
Hollytrees. GU13—5H 29
Holly Way. GU17—2G 9
Holmbrook Gdns. GU14—3F 15
Holt Clo. GU14—4D 16
Holt Pound Cotts. GU10—6A 26
Holt Pound La. GU10—5A 26
Holyfields Clo. GU15—1A 10
Holywell Clo. GU14—7K 9
Home Farm Clo. GU14—1C 16
Homelea Clo. GU14—6A 10
Homeleigh Cres. GU12—7F 17
Home Pk. GU17—7A 2
Homepark Ho. GU9—7F 23
Hone Hill. GU17—5E 2
Honeysuckle Clo. GU17—3C 28
Honister Gdns. GU14—5B 14
Honister Wlk. GU15—2J 11
Hook La. GU24—7D 6
Hook Mill La. GU18—3E 6
Hookstile La. GU9—1F 27
Hookstone La. GU24—5G 7
Hope Grant's Rd. GU11—4K 19

Hope La. GU9—3E 22
Hopeman Clo. GU15—6G 3
Hormer Clo. GU15—4G 3
Hornbeam Clo. GU14—2F 15
Hornbeam Clo. GU15—4G 3
Horn Rd. GU14—2H 15
Horsebrass Dri. GU19—3K 5
Horseshoe Clo. GU15—5E 4
Horseshoe Cres. GU15—5E 4
Horseshoe La. GU12—1F 21
Horsham Rd. GU15—4G 3
Hospital Hill. GU11—5K 19
Hospital Rd. GU11—5K 19
Hostel Rd. GU14—7A 16
Houlton Ct. GU19—3K 5
Houseman Rd. GU14—1J 15
Howard Clo. GU12—1F 21
Howard Cole Way. GU11
—6H 19
Howes Gdns. GU13—5H 29
Huddington Glade. GU17
—4C 28
Humber Way. GU17—5G 3
Humphrey Pk. GU15—7J 29
(in two parts)
Hungerford Clo. GU17—5F 3
Hunter Rd. GU14—4J 15
Hunts La. GU15—4A 10
Huntsmans M. GU16—4E 16
Hurlands Clo. GU9—5J 23
Hurst Rd. GU11—4B 20
Hurst Rd. GU14—6A 10
Hussar Ct. GU11—5H 19
Hutton Clo. GU20—2E 6
Hutton Rd. GU12—2F 21

Iberian Way. GU15—7F 5
I.A.M. Rd. GU14—7A 16
Ilex Clo. GU17—3D 28
Imjin Clo. GU15—7J 29
Ingle Dell. GU15—2C 10
Inglewood Av. GU15—2H 11
Inner Quadrant. GU12—3E 20
Innisfail Gdns. GU11—1J 23
Institute Rd. GU11—5B 20
Institute Rd. GU12—7C 20
Instow Gdns. GU14—7K 9
Inverness Way. GU15—6G 3
Invincible Rd. GU14—5K 15
Iris Dri. GU24—2H 13
Iris Rd. GU24—2H 13
Irvine Dri. GU14—6H 9
Isis Way. GU15—5G 3
Ively Rd. GU14—7D 14
Ives Clo. GU17—2D 28
Ivydene. GU21—5J 13
Ivy Dri. GU18—6B 6
Ivy La. GU9—7E 22
Ivy Rd. GU12—6C 20

James Rd. GU15—4A 10
James Way. GU15—4A 10
Jarvis Clo. RG27—1A 28
Jay Clo. GU20—1F 7
Jays Nest Clo. GU17—2G 9
Jean Orr Ct. GU15—5B 4
Jefferson Rd. GU24—7D 12
Jenkins Pl. GU14—7C 16
Jenkyns Hill. GU19—3J 5
Jenner Dri. GU24—7H 7
Jennys Wlk. GU17—7B 2
Jersey Clo. GU13—3A 14
Jesse Clo. GU17—1C 8
John Clo. GU11—1H 23
Johnson Way. GU13—6K 29
Jubilee Clo. GU14—3G 15
Jubilee Ct. GU12—2F 21
Jubilee Hall Rd. GU14—3B 16
Jubilee La. GU10—6D 26
Jubilee Rd. GU11—2A 24
Jubilee Rd. GU16—5F 17
Junction Rd. GU18—4C 6
Juniper Dri. GU24—2H 13

Juniper Rd. GU14—2F 15

Keable Rd. GU10—3C 26
Keats Way. GU17—5D 28
Keble Way. GU15—3H 3
Keith Lucas Rd. GU14—5J 15
Kelsey Gro. GU17—1B 8
Kemp Ct. GU19—3A 6
Kendal Clo. GU14—3H 15
Kendal Gro. GU15—2J 11
Kenilworth Cres. GU13—5B 14
Kenilworth Rd. GU13—6A 14
Kenilworth Rd. GU14—2F 15
Kenmore Clo. GU13—3A 18
Kenmore Clo. GU16—6C 10
Kennel La. GU10—7F 27
Kennel La. GU13 & GU14—4E 14
Kennet Clo. GU12—7F 21
Kennet Clo. GU14—1H 15
Kentigern Dri. RG11—1G 3
Kenton Clo. GU16—4E 10
Kent Rd. GU13—6A 14
Kent Rd. GU20—1E 6
Kenwith Av. GU13—6B 14
Keogh Barracks. GU12—6G 17
Keogh Clo. GU12—6G 17
Kepple Pl. GU19—2K 5
Kerry Clo. GU13—3A 14
Kestrel Clo. GU10—2A 22
Keswick Clo. GU15—2J 11
Keswick Dri. GU18—5C 6
Kevins Dri. GU17—6B 2
Kevins Gro. GU13—6A 14
Keynes Clo. GU13—4A 18
Keynsham Way. GU15—3G 3
Kielder Wlk. GU15—2H 11
Kilmartin Gdns. GU16—5E 10
Kilmore Dri. GU15—2G 11
Kilmuir Clo. GU15—6G 3
Kiln La. GU10—4F 27
Kiln La. GU21—4J 13
Kiln Way. GU11—2A 24
Kimberley. GU13—4A 18
Kimbers La. GU9—6G 23
Kingcup Dri. GU24—2H 13
Kingfisher Clo. GU13—6K 29
Kingfisher Clo. GU15—2H 11
Kingfisher Dri. GU17—3D 28
Kingfisher Wlk. GU12—6E 20
Kings Av. GU10—1D 24
King's Av. GU24—6E 12
Kingsclear Pk. GU15—2C 10
King's Cres. GU15—5B 4
Kingscroft. GU13—3K 29
Kings Keep. GU13—5K 29
Kings Keep. GU17—4E 2
Kings La. GU10—4C 26
Kings La. GU20—1F 7
Kingsley Av. GU15—2B 10
Kingsley Clo. RG11—2E 2
Kingsley Rd. GU14—1J 15
Kingsmead. GU14—3A 16
Kingsmead. GU16—7D 10
Kingsmead Shopping Centre.
GU14—4A 16
Kings Pde. GU13—2K 29
Kings Ride. GU15—4C 4
King's Rd. GU11—7H 19
Kings Rd. GU13—1K 29
King's Rd. GU14—1H 13
King's Rd. RG11—1E 2
Kingston Rd. GU15—5F 5
King's Wlk. GU11—7H 19
Kingsway. GU11—7H 19
Kingsway. GU17—1C 8
Kipling Clo. GU17—5E 28
Kirkham Clo. GU15—3G 3
Kirkstone Clo. GU15—2J 11
Kirriemuir Gdns. GU12—5J 21
Kitchener Rd. GU11—7F 19
Knightsbridge Gro. GU15—6D 4
Knightsbridge Rd. GU15—6D 4
Knights Rd. GU9—2H 23
Knoll Clo. GU13—1K 29
Knoll Rd. GU13—1K 29

Knoll Rd. GU15—7C 4
Knoll Wlk. GU15—7C 4
Knollys Rd. GU11—5J 19
Kohat Ct. GU11—6J 19
Kohima Clo. GU11—5A 20
Krooner Rd. GU15—3A 10

Laburnum Clo. GU11—7K 19
Laburnum Pl. GU11—7K 19
Laburnum Rd. GU9—2H 23
Laburnum Rd. GU11—7K 19
Ladywood Av. GU14—3F 15
Laffan's Rd. GU11—2F 19
Laird Ct. GU19—4K 5
Lake End. RG11—1D 2
Lakeland Dri. GU16—5D 10
Lake Rd. GU16—1F 17
Lakeside Clo. GU12—3E 20
Lakeside Gdns. GU14—1H 15
Lakeside Rd. GU12—4E 20
Lakeside, The. GU17—2G 9
Lambert Cres. GU17—2F 9
Lamborne Clo. GU17—4D 2
Lambourne Dri. GU19—3J 5
Lambourne Way. GU10—2D 24
Lanark Clo. GU16—4D 10
Lancaster Av. GU9—2F 27
Lancaster Way. GU14—7B 10
Lancer Ct. GU11—6H 19
Landseer Clo. GU17—7H 3
Lane End Dri. GU21—4K 13
Langdale Clo. GU14—3H 15
Langdon Clo. GU15—2H 11
Langham Ct. GU9—3F 27
Langley Clo. GU13—7J 29
Langley Dri. GU15—7J 29
Lansdowne Rd. GU11—7K 19
Lansdowne Rd. GU16—6F 11
Larch Clo. GU15—5D 4
Larchfield Rd. GU13—4K 29
Larch Way. GU14—4F 15
Larch Way. GU17—1E 8
Larchwood Glade. GU15—6F 5
Larkfield Clo. GU9—6C 22
Larkfield Rd. GU9—6C 22
Larkspur Clo. GU11—2K 23
Larks Way. GU21—3K 13
Larkswood Clo. GU17—4D 2
Larmer Clo. GU13—4G 29
Latchwood La. GU10—5G 27
Latham Av. GU16—4D 10
Lauder Clo. GU16—4D 10
Laundry La. GU15—1J 9
Laurel Clo. GU14—4F 15
Laurel Clo. GU15—2C 10
Laurel Gro. GU10—5C 26
Laurels, The. GU9—2J 23
Laurels, The. GU13—2K 29
Lavender La. GU10—6C 26
Lawday Link. GU9—2D 22
Lawday Pl. GU9—2D 22
Lawday Pl. La. GU9—2D 22
Lawford Cres. GU17—7A 2
Lawrence Cres. GU20—1E 6
Lawrence Rd. GU13—3J 29
Lawrence Way. GU15—2J 9
Laws Ter. GU11—5B 20
Lea Clo. GU9—3K 23
Lea Clo. GU12—7F 21
Lea Ct. GU9—2J 23
Lea La. GU13—4H 29
Lea Rd. GU15—4A 10
Lea Springs. GU13—4G 29
Lea, The. GU13—4G 29
Lea Way. GU12—5E 20
Leawood Rd. GU13—4H 29
Lee Ct. GU11—1B 24
Lee Rd. GU11—6H 19
Legge Cres. GU11—7H 19
Leigh La. GU9—2H 27
Leipzig Rd. GU13—5A 18
Le Marchant Rd. GU15—3E 10
Lendore Rd. GU16—6C 10
Lennel Gdns. GU13—2B 18
Leonard Clo. GU16—6C 10

Leopold Av. GU14—2A 16
Lestock Way. GU13—6B 14
Levern Dri. GU15—4G 3
Lewisham Way. GU15—4G 3
Ley Rd. GU14—6K 9
Ley Side. RG11—1D 2
Lickfolds Rd. GU10—7B 26
Lightwater By-Pass. GU18
—3B 6
Lightwater Meadow. GU18
—5C 6
Lightwater Rd. GU18—5C 6
Lille Barracks. GU11—1C 20
Lime Av. GU15—7F 5
Lime Cres. GU12—6G 21
Limecroft. GU17—4E 28
Limecroft Rd. GU12—4J 13
Limes Rd. GU14—2F 15
Lime St. GU11—6J 19
Lincoln Clo. GU15—2G 11
Lindale Rd. GU15—3G 3
Linden Ct. GU15—6E 4
Lindens, The. GU9—2G 27
Lindum Clo. GU11—7K 19
Lindum Dene. GU11—7K 19
Ling Dri. GU18—6A 6
Lingmala Gro. GU13—3A 18
Links Way. GU14—4F 15
Link, The. GU17—3E 28
Linkway. GU13—5J 29
Linkway. GU15—2B 10
Linkway. RG11—1C 2
Linkway Pde. GU13—5J 29
Linsford La. GU16—4E 16
Linstead Rd. GU14—6H 9
Lion & Lamb Way. GU9—7E 22
Lion & Lamb Yd. GU9—7E 22
Lion Way. GU13—3A 18
Liskeard Dri. GU14—1K 15
Lismoyne Clo. GU13—1J 29
Lit. Austins Rd. GU9—2G 27
Lit. Copse. GU13—4H 29
Lit. Copse. GU17—6A 2
Littlefield Clo. GU12—7F 21
Littlefield Gdns. GU12—7F 21
Lit. Green La. GU9—3D 26
Lit. Moor. GU17—4F 3
Lit. Paddock. GU5—5F 5
Lit. Thurbans Clo. GU9—4D 26
Lit. Vigo. GU17—5D 28
Lit. Wellington St. GU11
—6K 19
Littleworth Rd. GU10—7D 24
Llangar Gro. RG11—1D 2
Lobelia Rd. GU24—2H 13
Lockswood. GU24—7J 13
Lockwood Clo. GU14—6H 9
Loddon Clo. GU15—7F 5
Loddon Rd. GU14—1G 15
Loddon Way. GU12—7F 21
Lodge Clo. GU11—1B 24
Lodge Gro. GU17—7C 2
Lodge Hill Clo. GU10—4G 27
Lodge Hill Rd. GU10—4G 27
Loman Rd. GU16—4F 17
London Rd. GU16, GU15, GU19,
GU20, SL5, GU2—7E 28
London Rd. GU17—7A 28
London Rd. RG27, GU17, GU15 &
GU19—7A 28
Loneacre. GU20—1F 7
Longacre. GU12—6F 21
Long Beech Dri. GU14—4F 15
Long Bri. GU9—7F 23
Longdown. GU13—5J 29
Longdown Clo. GU10—4F 27
Longdown Rd. GU10—5E 26
Longdown Rd. GU17—4D 2
Longfield Clo. GU14—6K 9
Longfield Rd. GU12—6F 21
Longford Clo. GU15—2C 10
Long Garden Wlk. GU9—7E 22
Long Garden Wlk. E. GU9
—6E 22
Long Garden Wlk. W. GU9
—6E 22
Long Garden Way. GU9—7E 22

Longhope Dri. GU10—4D 26
Longlands Way. GU15—1J 11
Longleat Sq. GU14—4D 16
Longley Rd. GU9—1G 27
Longmead. GU13—5K 29
Longmeadow. GU16—3E 10
Long Mickle. GU11—4D 2
Long Rd., The. GU10—7C 26
Long Wlk. GU9—6E 22
Longwater La. RG27—1A 28
Longwater Rd. RG27—1B 28
Lorraine Rd. GU15—5E 4
Lothian Rd. GU24—7B 12
Louise Margaret Rd. GU11
—5B 20
Lovelands La. GU24—7K 7
Love La. GU12—6C 21
Love La. GU17—3C 28
Lovells Clo. GU18—4C 6
Lwr. Broadmoor Rd. RG11
—1F 3
Lwr. Charles St. GU15—7B 4
Lwr. Church La. GU9—7E 22
Lwr. Church Rd. GU17—4B 2
Lwr. Farnham Rd. GU11 & GU12
—2A 24
Lwr. Guildford Rd. GU21
—4K 13
Lwr. Mill Field. GU19—3J 5
Lwr. Nelson St. GU11—6K 19
Lwr. Newport Rd. GU12—7C 20
Lwr. Sandhurst Rd. RG11 &
GU17—3A 2
Lwr. South View. GU9—6F 23
—3J 23
Lwr. Weybourne La. GU9
Lwr. Wokingham Rd. RG11
—1A 2
Loweswater Wlk. GU15—2J 11
Lowlands Rd. GU17—2F 9
Low La. GU9—3A 24
Lowndes Bldgs. GU9—6E 22
Lowry Clo. GU17—7G 3
Loxwood Av. GU13—4H 29
Lucas Clo. GU17—1A 8
Lucas Dri. GU17—1A 8
Lucas Grn. Rd. GU24—2E 12
Ludlow Clo. GU16—7F 11
Luke Rd. GU11—1H 23
Luke Rd. E. GU11—1H 23
Lulworth Clo. GU14—7K 9
Lupin Clo. GU19—4H 5
Lyall Pl. GU9—2E 22
Lych Ga. Clo. GU17—5C 2
Lydford Clo. GU14—7K 9
Lydford Clo. GU16—7F 11
Lye Copse Av. GU14—6A 10
Lymington Av. GU17—4D 28
Lynchford La. GU14—6D 16
Lynchford Rd. GU11—1A 20
Lynch Rd. GU9—7G 23
Lyndale Clo. GU13—6C 14
Lyndford Ter. GU13—4J 29
Lyndhurst Av. GU11—3B 24
Lyndhurst Av. GU17—7F 3
Lynn Rd. GU14—7J 9
Lynwood Dri. GU16—4F 17
Lyon Way. GU16—5B 10
Lysons Av. GU17—7E 16
Lyson's Rd. GU11—7K 19

Macdonald Rd. GU9—2E 22
Macdonald Rd. GU18—6A 6
McGrigor Barracks. GU11
—5A 20
McKay Clo. GU11—5B 20
McKernan Ct. GU15—5C 2
McNaughton Clo. GU14—4F 15
Macrae Rd. GU17—3E 28
Madeley Rd. GU13—2A 18
Magdalene Rd. GU13—3J 3
Magnolia Clo. GU15—4G 3
Magnolia Way. GU13—4K 29
Magpie Clo. GU10—1A 22
Maguire Dri. GU16—3H 11
Maida Rd. GU11—4A 20

Paddock, The. GU18—5C 6
Pannells. GU10—5G 27
Pan's Gdns. GU15—2E 10
Parade, The. GU12—4F 21
Parade, The. GU17—1B 8
Parfitts Clo. GU9—7D 22
Parish Clo. GU12—4F 21
Parish Rd. GU14—7B 16
Park Av. GU15—2B 10
Park Ct. GU9—6G 23
Park Farm Ind. Est. GU15
—5B 10
Park Hill. GU13—6J 29
Parkhill Clo. GU17—2G 9
Parkhill Rd. GU17—2G 9
Parkland Gro. GU9—1J 23
Park La. GU15—1B 10
Park Pl. GU13—6J 29
Park Rd. GU9—5G 23
Park Rd. GU11—1A 24
Park Rd. GU14—6D 16
Park Rd. GU15—3A 10
Park Rd. GU17—6F 3
Park Row. GU9—6E 22
Parkside. GU9—3F 23
Parkstone Dri. GU14—5F 15
Park St. GU15—7B 4
Park St. GU19—2K 5
Park View. GU19—2J 5
Parkway. GU15—3B 10
Parkway. RG11—1D 2
Parliamentary Rd. GU24
—7B 12
Parnham Av. GU18—5E 6
Parsonage Way. GU16—5D 10
Parsons Clo. GU13—6J 29
Parsons Cotts. GU14—5H 21
Parsons Field. GU17—5E 2
Partridge Av. GU17—3D 28
Partridge Clo. GU14—1A 22
Partridge Clo. GU16—5D 10
Paschal Rd. GU15—5E 4
Pathfinders, The. GU14—4F 15
Patten Av. GU17—4E 28
Patterson Clo. GU16—3H 11
Paul Clo. GU11—1H 23
Paul's Field. RG27—1A 28
Pavilion La. GU11—6H 19
Pavilion Rd. GU11—7H 19
Paviours. GU9—6E 22
Peabody Rd. GU14—6C 16
Pear Tree La. GU10—7C 26
Peatmoor Clo. GU13—1H 29
Peddlars Gro. GU17—7B 2
Peel Av. GU16—7F 11
Pegasus Av. GU12—5D 20
Pegasus Rd. GU14—7J 9
Peggotty Pl. GU15—3H 3
Pembroke B'way. GU15—1B 10
Pembroke Pde. GU17—7B 2
Pembury Pl. GU12—7B 20
Pendragon Way. GU15—2J 11
Penfold Croft. GU9—5J 23
(in two parts)
Pennefathers Rd. GU11—5J 19
Pennine Way. GU14—7G 9
Penns Wood. GU14—6C 16
Pennypot La. GU24—6K 7
Penshurst Rise. GU10—6E 10
Pentland Pl. GU14—7H 9
Perowne St. GU11—6A 20
Perring Av. GU14—6H 9
Perry Dri. GU13—2G 29
Perryhill Dri. GU17—4C 2
Perry Way. GU18—6A 6
Peterhouse Clo. GU15—3J 3
Petworth Clo. GU16—6E 10
Pevensey Way. GU16—6F 11
Pheasant Copse. GU13—1G 29
Pickford St. GU11—6A 20
Pierrefonde's Av. GU14—2K 15
Pike Clo. GU11—6B 20
Pilcot Rd. GU13—5F 29
Pilgrims Clo. GU9—2D 26
Pilgrims View. GU12—1H 25
Pilgrims Way. GU24—3H 13

Pine Av. GU15—2C 10
Pine Clo. GU12—2F 21
Pine Clo. GU15—6H 3
Pine Ct. GU11—6K 19
Pine Dri. GU17—3H 9
Pinefields Clo. RG11—1E 2
Pine Gro. GU10—4H 27
Pine Gro. GU13—3A 18
Pine Gro. GU20—1E 6
Pinehill Rise. GU17—5F 3
Pinehill Rd. RG11—1E 2
Pinehurst Av. GU14—5A 16
Pinehurst Cotts. GU14—5A 16
Pinehurst Ga. Path. GU14
—5A 16
(off O'Gorman Av.)
Pine Mt. Rd. GU15—2C 10
Pine Ridge Dri. GU10—5E 26
Pines Rd. GU13—1J 29
Pine View Clo. GU9—4K 23
Pinewood Ct. GU13—1K 29
Pinewood Cres. GU14—2F 15
Pinewood Gdns. GU19—2H 5
Pinewood Hill. GU13—1K 29
Pinewood Pk. GU14—7F 9
Pinewood Rd. GU12—5J 21
Pipers Croft. GU13—7K 29
Pipson La. GU17—1A 8
Pirbright Rd. GU3—5K 21
Pirbright Rd. GU14—4B 16
Pitt Way. GU14—2J 15
Place Ct. GU11—2B 24
Plantation Row. GU15—1A 10
Plough Rd. GU17—6B 2
Plover Rise. GU14—7F 13
Polden Clo. GU14—7H 9
Polkerris Way. GU13—4A 18
Pollard Gro. GU15—2H 11
Polmear Clo. GU13—4A 18
Pond Croft. GU17—7B 2
Pondtail Gdns. GU13—7B 14
Pondtail Rd. GU13—7B 14
Pool Rd. GU11—2B 24
Poplar Clo. GU14—2F 15
Poplar Clo. GU14—4F 17
Poplar Wlk. GU9—2G 23
Poppyhills Rd. GU15—5E 4
Portesbery Hill Dri. GU15—7D 4
Portesbery Rd. GU15—7C 4
Portland Dri. GU13—7J 29
Portsmouth Rd. GU16 & GU15
—5C 10
Port Way. GU24—3H 13
Potley Hill Rd. GU17—7C 2
Potteries La. GU16—4E 16
Potteries, The. GU14—1G 15
Potters Cres. GU12—5G 21
Potters Ga. GU9—7D 22
Potters Ind. Pk. GU13—3B 18
Pottery Ct. GU10—4C 26
Pottery La. GU10—4C 26
Pound Farm La. GU12—6J 21
Pound La. GU20—1D 6
Pound Rd. GU12—7B 20
Powderham St. GU11—6A 20
Poyle Rd. GU10—2E 24
Prentice Clo. GU14—6A 10
Priest La. GU24—7D 6
Primrose Av. GU24—2H 13
Primrose Wlk. GU13—1J 29
Primrose Wlk. GU17—3D 28
Primrose Way. GU17—4E 2
Prince Charles Cres. GU14
—6A 10
Prince Dri. GU12—5H 21
Prince of Wales Wlk. GU15
—7B 4
Prince's Av. GU11—3A 20
Princess Way. GU15—7B 4
Princes Way. GU19—4K 5
Prior Croft Clo. GU15—2F 11
Prior End. GU15—1F 11
Prior Rd. GU15—1F 11
Priors Clo. GU14—6K 9
Priors Ct. GU12—7D 20
Priors Keep. GU13—7A 14

Prior's La. GU17—1D 8
Priors Wood. RG11—1A 2
Priory Clo. GU13—3G 29
Priory St. GU14—3C 16
Prospect Av. GU14—1A 16
Prospect Rd. GU10—7B 26
Prospect Rd. GU12—3F 21
Prospect Rd. GU14—3K 15
Purley Way. GU16—6D 10
Puttenham Rd. GU10—5G 25
Pyestock Cres. GU14—3F 15

Quadrant, The. GU12—4F 21
Quarry La. GU17—1B 8
Quarters Rd. GU14—5A 16
Quebec Gdns. GU17—2G 9
Queen Elizabeth Barracks. GU13
—7K 29
Queen Elizabeth Dri. GU11
—6J 19
Queen Elizabeth Rd. GU15
—4C 4
Queen Mary Av. GU15—1K 9
Queen's Av. GU11—5K 19
Queensbury Pl. GU17—3F 9
Queens Clo. GU14—7A 16
Queens Clo. GU24—3H 13
Queen's Ct. GU14—7B 16
Queens La. GU9—2F 23
Queensmead. GU14—3A 16
Queen's Pde. Path. GU11
—2A 20
Queens Rd. GU9—3F 23
Queen's Rd. GU11—7J 19
Queen's Rd. GU13—4K 29
Queen's Rd. GU14—7B 16
Queens Rd. GU15—2A 10
Queen's Rd. GU21—5K 13
Queens Rd. GU24—7F 13
Queen St. GU12—6C 20
Queensway. GU16—7F 11
Queen's Way. GU24—6E 12
Queen Victoria Rd. GU24
—6E 12
Queen Victoria's Wlk. GU15
—7J 3
Quennells Hill. GU10—4B 26
Quetta Pk. GU13—6A 18
Quince Dri. GU24—2J 13
Quinney's. GU14—6B 16

Rackstraw Rd. GU15—4F 3
Radcliffe Clo. GU16—7E 10
Radford Clo. GU9—4H 23
Raeburn Way. GU15—7G 3
Rafborough Footpath. GU14
—4K 15
Raglan Clo. GU12—5H 21
Raglan Clo. GU16—6F 11
Ramillies Pk. GU11—1D 20
Ramillies Rd. GU11—1B 20
Ramsay Rd. GU20—1F 7
Randell Clo. GU17—5H 9
Randell Ho. GU17—5H 9
Range Ride. GU15—6J 3
Range View. GU15—5H 3
Rankine Clo. GU14—3B 16
Rapallo Clo. GU14—3B 16
Rapley Clo. GU15—5E 4
Rashleigh Ct. GU13—4A 18
Ratcliffe Rd. GU14—6J 9
Raven Clo. GU17—3D 28
Ravens Clo. GU21—3K 13
Ravenscroft Clo. GU12—5H 21
Ravenstone Rd. GU15—1J 11
Ravenswood Av. RG11—1B 2
Ravenswood Dri. GU15—1F 11
Ravesby Clo. GU24—7E 6
Rawlinson Rd. GU15—7K 3
Reading Rd. GU13—6B 16
Reading Rd. GU17—2D 28
(Yateley)
Reading Rd. RG27—1A 28
Reading Rd. N. GU13—1G 29
Reading Rd. S. GU13—3J 29

Recreation Rd. GU10—7B 26
Rectory Clo. GU17—5C 2
Rectory La. GU20—1D 6
Rectory Rd. GU14—3B 16
Redan Gdns. GU12—6B 20
Redan Rd. GU12—6B 20
Redcrest Gdns. GU15—1E 10
Rede Ct. GU14—6B 16
Redfields La. GU13—7J 29
Red Lion La. GU9—1E 26
Redmayne Clo. GU15—2H 11
Red Rd. GU18—7J 5
Redvers Buller Rd. GU11
—1B 20
Redwood Dri. GU15—2J 11
Redwoods Way. GU13—3A 18
Reeds Rd., The. GU10—7J 27
Reeves Rd. GU12—7B 20
Regent Clo. GU13—3K 29
Regent Ct. GU19—3A 6
Regents Pl. GU17—5F 3
Regent St. GU13—3K 29
Regent Way. GU16—5E 10
Regiment Clo. GU14—4F 15
Reidonhill Cotts. GU21—5J 13
Retreat, The. GU15—5H 29
Revelstoke Av. GU14—1A 16
Reynolds Way. GU15—7G 3
Rhine Banks. GU14—2G 15
Rhine Barracks. GU11—5K 19
Rhododendron Rd. GU16
—6F 11
Ribble Pl. GU14—1H 15
Richard Clo. GU13—4H 29
Richmond Clo. GU13—5J 29
Richmond Clo. GU16—5E 10
Richmond Rd. GU15—5H 3
Rideway Clo. GU15—2A 10
Ridgemount Est. GU16—7H 11
Ridgeway Pde. GU13—6K 29
Ridgeway, The. GU24—7H 13
Ridgway Hill Rd. GU9—2F 27
Ridgway Rd. GU9—3F 27
Ridings, The. GU16—3G 11
Ridley Clo. GU13—4H 29
Rifle Way. GU14—4F 15
Rimbault Clo. GU11—1C 20
Ringwood Rd. GU14—7B 10
Ringwood Rd. GU17—7F 3
Ripon Clo. GU15—3J 11
Ripplesmore Clo. GU17—5E 2
Rise, The. RG11—1C 2
Riverdale. GU10—3B 26
River La. GU10—3B 26
Rivermead Rd. GU15—4A 10
River Rd. GU17—1D 28
River Row Cotts. GU10—3C 26
Rivers Clo. GU14—6D 16
Riverside Av. GU18—4D 6
Riverside Clo. GU14—2J 15
Riverside Clo. GU24—7G 13
Riverside Pk. GU15—3K 9
Riverside Pk. Ind. Est. GU9
—6G 23
Riverside Way. GU15—3K 9
Robertson Way. GU12—7B 20
Roberts Rd. GU12—7B 20
Roberts Rd. GU15—7K 3
Robert Way. GU16—4E 16
Robin Clo. GU12—2F 21
Robin Hill Dri. GU15—3F 11
Robin Hood Clo. GU14—7K 9
Robin La. GU17—5E 2
Robin's Bow. GU15—2A 10
Robins Dale. GU21—4K 13
Robins Gro. Cres. GU17—3D 28
Rochester Gro. GU13—3K 29
Rockfield Way. GU15—5G 3
Rock Gdns. GU11—7J 19
Rock La. GU10—3B 26
Rokes Pl. GU17—3C 28
Roman Ride. RG11—1A 2
Roman Way. GU9—5H 23
Romany Rd. GU21—2K 13
Romayne Clo. GU14—2K 15
Romsey Clo. GU11—3B 24

Romsey Clo. GU17—7F 3
Rookwood Av. GU15—3H 3
Rorkes Drift. GU16—3E 16
Rosary Gdns. GU17—7A 2
Rosebury Dri. GU24—2H 13
Rosedene Gdns. GU13—1J 29
Rosedene La. GU15—7G 3
Rosemary Av. GU12—7F 17
Rosemary Clo. GU14—3G 15
Rosemary Gdns. GU17—1F 9
Rosemary La. GU10—6B 26
Rosemary La. GU17—7F 3
Rose Wlk. GU13—1J 29
Rosewood Way. GU24—7G 7
Rossmore Gdns. GU11—7H 19
Rothbury Wlk. GU15—2H 11
Rother Clo. GU17—5F 3
Rother Rd. GU14—1H 15
Rotherwick Ct. GU14—7B 16
Rothwell Ho. RG11—1F 3
Rotunda Est. GU12—6A 20
Rounce La. GU24—7E 6
Round Clo. GU17—1C 8
Roundway. GU15—7H 5
Roundway Clo. GU15—7H 5
Rounton Rd. GU13—5K 29
Rowan Chase. GU10—5D 26
Rowan Clo. GU13—6B 14
Rowan Clo. GU15—5E 4
Rowans Clo. GU14—5H 9
Rowcroft Clo. GU12—2F 21
Rowhill Av. GU17—1G 9
Rowhill Cres. GU11—1J 23
Rowhills. GU9—1G 23
Roxburgh Clo. GU15—2H 11
Royal Aerospace Establishment.
GU14—5A 16
Royale Ct. GU14—1B 24
Rudd Hall Rise. GU15—7C 10
Rufford Clo. GU13—5K 29
Rugby Clo. GU15—4H 3
Runwick La. GU10—1A 26
Rushden Way. GU9—2G 23
Rushmoor Clo. GU13—4K 29
Rushmoor Ct. GU14—7B 16
Rushmoor Rd. GU11—3G 19
Russell Ct. GU11—1G 9
Russet Clo. GU10—2D 24
Russet Gdns. GU15—3C 10
Russetts Dri. GU13—3K 29
Rutland Clo. GU11—5K 19
Rutland Ter. GU11—6K 19
Ryan Mt. GU17—5D 2
Rydal Clo. GU14—4G 15
Rydal Clo. GU15—1J 11
Rydal Dri. GU13—6H 29
Rydal Pl. GU18—5C 6
Ryde Gdns. GU17—3D 28
Ryebeck Rd. GU13—6K 29
Rye Clo. GU13—2B 14
Rye Clo. GU14—1H 15
Ryecroft Gdns. GU17—2H 9
Rye Gro. GU24—2G 7
Ryeland Clo. GU13—3B 14
Ryelaw Rd. GU13—6K 29
Ryle Rd. GU9—2E 26
Ryvers Av. GU17—4C 28

Sabre Ct. GU11—6H 19
Saddleback Rd. GU15—5D 4
Saddleback Way. GU13—3A 14
Saddlewood. GU15—2B 10
Saffron Ct. GU14—3F 15
St Andrew's Way. GU16—7E 10
St Annes Glade. GU19—2J 5
St Augustine's Clo. GU12
—7C 20
St Benedicts Clo. GU11—7K 19
St-Catherines Rd. GU16—5E 10
St Christopher's Pl. GU14
—4J 15
St Christopher's Rd. GU14
—4K 15
St Clement's Ct. GU14—7A 10
St Cross Rd. GU9—6F 23
St Cross Rd. GU16—7F 11

St Davids Clo. GU9—2H 23
St David's Clo. GU14—6J 9
St Denys Clo. GU21—5K 13
St George's Clo. GU9—3A 24
St George's Ind. Est. GU15
—3A 10
St George's Rd. GU9—3A 24
(Badshot Lea)
St George's Rd. GU9—1G 27
(Farnham)
St George's Rd. GU12—7A 20
St George's Rd. GU15—7C 4
St George's Rd. E. GU12—7A 20
St Helens Cres. GU14—5E 2
St James' Av. GU9—6G 23
St James' Ct. GU9—6F 23
St James Rd. GU13—3J 29
St James' Ter. GU9—6F 23
St John's Ct. GU24—7G 13
St John's Rd. GU9—2E 26
St John's Rd. GU14—2H 15
St John's Rd. GU17—6E 2
St Joseph's Rd. GU12—7K 19
St Mark's Clo. GU14—6B 16
St Marks Pl. GU9—2E 22
St Mary's Clo. GU17—5F 3
St Mary's Gdns. GU19—2K 5
St Mary's Rd. GU12—3F 21
St Mary's Rd. GU15—7B 4
St Michaels Clo. GU13—7A 14
St Michael's Rd. GU12—7A 20
St Michael's Rd. GU14—1A 16
St Michael's Rd. GU15—1A 10
St Michael's Rd. GU17—5C 2
St Omer Barracks. GU11
—3C 20
St Peter's Gdns. GU17—7A 2
St Peters Mead. GU12—6G 21
St Peters Pk. GU11—1H 23
St Peter's Way. GU16—7E 10
St Philips Ct. GU13—2K 29
Salamanca. RG11—1B 2
Salamanca Pk. GU11—5J 19
Salerno Clo. GU14—5K 19
Sales Ct. GU11—7J 19
Salisbury Gro. GU16—3E 16
Salisbury Rd. GU15—5F 21
Salisbury Rd. GU14—3B 16
Salisbury Rd. GU17—2F 9
Salisbury Ter. GU16—4F 17
Saltram Rd. GU14—5D 16
Samarkand Clo. GU15—2G 11
Sampson's Almshouses. GU9
—1C 26
San Carlos App. GU11—6B 20
Sandford Ct. GU11—7J 19
Sandford Rd. GU9—2E 22
Sandford Rd. GU11—7J 19
Sand Hill. GU14—7A 10
Sand Hill Ct. GU14—7A 10
Sandhurst La. GU17—7E 2
Sandhurst Rd. GU17—7E 2
Sandhurst Rd. RG11—2E 2
(Crowthorne)
Sandown Clo. GU17—1G 9
Sandown Cres. GU11—2A 24
Sandown Dri. GU14—4C 10
Sandpit La. GU21—2K 13
Sandringham Way. GU16
—6E 10
Sandrock Hill Rd. GU10—4C 26
Sands Clo. GU10—7C 24
Sands Rd. GU10—6B 24
Sandy Hill Rd. GU9—2D 22
Sandy La. GU13—7K 29
Sandy La. GU14—1F 15
Sandy La. GU15—7D 4
Sandy La. GU17—4C 2
Sankey La. GU13—3C 14
Santina Clo. GU9—1G 23
Saunton Gdns. GU14—1K 15
Saville Gdns. GU15—1G 11
Savoy Clo. GU17—3G 9
Saxon Croft. GU9—1F 27
Sayers Clo. GU16—7D 10
Scarlett's Rd. GU11—5K 19
School Clo. GU24—2G 13

School Hill. GU10—5G 25
(Seale)
School Hill. GU10—3C 26
(Wrecclesham)
School Hill. GU14—4D 2
School Hill. RG11—1G 3
School La. GU10—1A 22
(Ewshot)
School La. GU10—4G 27
(Lower Bourne)
School La. GU17—3D 28
School La. GU19—3J 5
School La. GU20—1E 6
School Rd. GU10—7B 26
School Rd. GU20—1C 6
Scotland Clo. GU12—3F 21
Scotland Farm Rd. GU12
—3F 21
Scotland Hill. GU17—4D 2
Scott's Clo. GU14—7A 10
Scott's Gro. Clo. GU24—7K 7
Scott's Gro. Rd. GU24—7K 7
Scutley La. GU18—3F 7
Seale La. GU10—5C 24
Seale La. GU10 & GU3—5K 25
Searle La. GU9—2F 27
Seaton Rd. GU15—1A 10
Sebastopol Rd. GU11—6A 20
Sedgemoor. GU14—7A 10
Sefton Clo. GU24—7G 7
Selborne Av. GU11—2A 24
Selborne Clo. GU17—7F 3
Selwyn Dri. GU17—3D 28
Sett, The. GU17—4D 28
Severn Clo. GU17—5F 3
Severn Rd. GU14—1H 15
Seymour Ct. GU11—1K 29
Seymour Ct. RG11—1B 2
Shady Nook. GU9—3E 22
Shaftesbury Ct. GU14—7B 16
Shaftesbury Mt. GU17—3G 9
Shaftesbury Rd. GU24—3G 13
Shakespeare Gdns. GU14
—2G 15
Shalbourne Rise. GU15—1D 10
Shalden Rd. GU12—1C 24
Shaldons Way. GU13—3G 29
Shamrock Clo. GU16—6C 10
Shawfield Cotts. GU12—6E 20
Shawfield La. GU12—6E 20
Shawfield Rd. GU12—7E 20
Shaw Pk. RG11—2E 2
Sheephatch La. GU10—5K 27
Sheep Ho. GU9—2F 27
Sheet's Heath La. GU24—6E 6
Sheffield Rd. GU14—3J 15
Shelley Clo. GU13—3K 29
Shelley Wlk. GU17—4E 28
Shepherd & Flock Roundabout.
GU9—6H 23
Shepherds Chase. GU19—3K 5
Shepherds Wlk. GU14—7H 9
Shepherds Way. RG11—1B 2
Sheraton Clo. GU17—2H 9
Sherborne Rd. GU14—6C 16
Sheridan Rd. GU16—6C 10
Sherwin Cres. GU14—6A 10
Shetland Way. GU13—3A 14
Shildon Clo. GU13—3J 11
Ship All. GU14—1B 16
Ship La. GU14—1B 16
Shire Av. GU13—3B 14
Shire Clo. GU19—3K 5
Shire Ct. GU11—6H 19
Shires Way. GU17—6A 2
Shirley Pl. GU21—4K 13
Shoe La. GU24—2K 19
Shortdale Rd. GU11—3B 24
Shortheath Crest. GU9—4D 26
Shortheath Rd. GU9—4D 26
Short St. GU11—6K 19
Shrivenham Clo. GU15—5G 3
Shrubbs Hill. GU24—3K 7
Shrubbs La. GU10—6C 26
Shrublands Dri. GU18—5C 6
Sian Clo. GU13—3A 18
Sidings, The. GU11—5B 20

Sidlaws Rd. GU14—7G 9
Silver Birch Clo. GU13—6J 29
Silverdale. GU13—5K 29
Silver Dri. GU16—3H 11
Silver Glades. GU17—5E 28
Silver Hill. GU15—5H 3
Silver Pk. Clo. GU13—2A 18
Silverwood Dri. GU15—6F 5
Sine Clo. GU14—4A 10
Sinhurst Rd. GU15—2A 10
Six Bells Roundabout. GU9
—4H 23
Slade La. GU12—4J 21
Slade Rd. GU24—7E 12
Slim Clo. GU11—1D 20
Smithy's Grn. GU20—1E 6
Snailslynch. GU9—7G 23
Snowdon Rd. GU14—7H 9
Snowdrop Wlk. GU13—1J 29
(off Stockton Av.)
Snowdrop Way. GU24—4H 13
Solartron Rd. GU14—4A 16
Somerset Ct. GU14—6B 16
Somerset Rd. GU14—6B 16
Somerville Cres. GU17—7B 2
Sonninge Clo. GU15—5G 3
Sorrel Dri. GU18—6A 6
Southampton Clo. GU17—7F 3
Southampton St. GU14—7A 16
S. Atlantic Dri. GU11—5B 20
South Av. GU9—3G 23
Southby Dri. GU13—6A 14
Southcote Dri. GU15—1F 11
Southern Rd. GU15—7B 4
Southern Way. GU11—1F 27
S. Farm La. GU18—3B 6
South Gro. GU13—3B 14
Southlands Clo. GU12—7F 21
Southlands Rd. GU12—7F 21
South La. GU12—7G 21
S. Mall. GU13—2J 29
S. Meadow. RG11—2G 3
(in three parts)
Southmead Rd. GU11—1A 24
South Rd. GU12—4F 21
South Rd. GU24—3G 13
South Rd. RG11—2H 3
(Crowthorne)
S. Side. GU10—2E 24
South St. GU9—7F 23
South St. GU14—6D 16
South Wlk. GU12—6C 20
Southwark Clo. GU17—3E 28
Southwell Pk. Rd. GU15—1A 10
Southwick. GU19—4K 5
Southwood La. GU15—4C 14
Southwood Rd. GU14—4G 15
Sparrowhawk Clo. GU10
—2A 22
Sparrow Row. GU24—1J 7
Sparvell Rd. GU21—6J 13
Sparvell Way. GU15—7B 4
Spencer Clo. GU13—3B 18
Spencer Clo. GU16—1D 16
Spinney, The. GU13—3G 29
Spinney, The. GU15—7H 5
Spinney, The. GU17—6A 2
Spoil La. GU10—2E 24
Spokane Clo. GU11—1J 23
Springcross Av. GU17—3G 9
Springfield. GU18—5E 6
Springfield La. GU13—2H 29
Springfield Rd. GU12—3F 21
Springfield Rd. GU15—1F 11
Spring Gdns. GU14—7K 9
Spring Gdns. GU17—1H 9
Spring La. GU9—2D 22
Spring La. W. GU9—3D 22
Spring Woods. GU13—4J 29
Spring Woods. GU17—4F 3
Spruce Dri. GU18—6B 6
Spruce Way. GU13—6C 14
Spurs Ct. GU11—6H 19
Spur, The. GU21—5J 13
Square, The. GU15—7B 4
Square, The. GU18—4D 6
Square, The. GU19—2K 5

Squirrel Clo. GU17—5E 2
Stable Croft. GU19—3J 5
Stable View. GU17—6A 2
Staff College. GU15—7B 4
Staff College Rd. GU15—7K 3
Staff Rd. GU12—6B 20
Stake La. GU14—2K 15
Stamford Av. GU16—5E 10
Stanhope Rd. GU15—2J 9
Stanley Dri. GU14—4F 15
Stanton Dri. GU13—3H 29
Star La. GU12—6E 20
Star Post Rd. GU15—5D 4
Station App. GU12—1F 21
Station App. GU13—4A 14
Station App. GU14—3A 16
Station App. GU17—2H 9
Station Hill. GU9—7F 23
Station Rd. GU11—6A 20
Station Rd. GU14—3A 16
Station Rd. GU16—5B 10
Station Rd. GU19—1K 5
Station Rd. E. GU12—1E 20
Station Rd. W. GU12—7E 16
Station View. GU12—7F 17
Steeforth Copse. GU15—3H 3
Steele's Rd. GU11—4A 20
Steep Hill. GU24—2K 7
Stephendale Rd. GU9—5G 23
Stevens Hill. GU17—1B 8
Stewards Rise. GU10—3C 26
Stilwell Clo. GU17—7B 2
Stirling Clo. GU16—4D 10
Stockbridge Dri. GU11—3B 24
Stockbridge Way. GU17—2A 8
Stockton Av. GU13—1J 29
Stockton Rd. GU13—1J 29
Stockwood Glades. GU9—2J 23
Stockwood Rise. GU15—1E 10
Stockwood Way. GU9—2J 23
Stoke Hills. GU9—6F 23
Stonegate. GU15—7H 5
Stonehill Rd. GU18—4B 6
Stonehouse Rise. GU16—5D 10
Stoneleigh Ct. GU16—5E 10
Stone St. GU12—7A 20
Stoney Clo. GU17—2A 8
Stoneyfields. GU9—1F 27
Stookes Way. GU17—5D 28
Stourhead Clo. GU14—3C 16
Stovold's Way. GU11—1J 23
Stratford Ct. GU9—2F 27
Stratford Rd. GU12—1C 24
Strathmore Ct. GU15—7C 4
Stratton Wlk. GU14—7K 9
Strawberry La. GU24—7E 12
Strawberry Field. GU24—3H 13
Strawberry Rise. GU24—2H 13
Stream Farm Clo. GU10—3G 27
Streamside. GU13—3K 29
Stream Valley Rd. GU10—4F 27
Streets Heath. GU24—6G 7
(in two parts)
Street, The. GU10—4E 24
(Tongham)
Street, The. GU10—3C 26
(Wrecclesham)
Street, The. GU13—6G 29
Stroud La. GU13—4F 29
Stuart Clo. GU14—2K 15
Stubbs Folly. GU15—6G 3
Stubbs Moor Rd. GU14—2J 15
Sturdee Clo. GU16—5D 10
Sturt Rd. GU12—2E 22
Sturt Rd. GU16—2E 16
Suffolk Clo. GU19—3K 5
Sullivan Clo. GU14—3A 16
Sullivan Rd. GU15—1K 9
Summerfield La. GU10—7E 26
Summer Gdns. GU15—1H 11
Summit Av. GU13 & GU14
—3E 4
Sumner Ct. GU9—6F 23
Sumner Rd. GU9—6F 23
Sunnybank Rd. GU14—1G 15
Sunnydell La. GU10—4D 26
Sunny Hill Rd. GU11—6G 19

Sunnyside. GU13—1H 29
Sunny View Clo. GU12—7B 20
Sun Ray Est. GU17—5D 2
Surbiton Rd. GU15—4F 5
Surrey Av. GU15—2K 9
Surridge Clo. GU19—3K 5
Sussex Clo. GU21—5K 13
Sussex Ct. GU21—4K 13
Sussex Gdns. GU13—3A 14
Sussex Rd. GU21—5K 13
Sutton Rd. GU15—4F 5
Swaledale Gdns. GU15—3A 14
Swale Rd. GU14—1H 15
Swallow Clo. GU17—3D 28
Swallow Rise. GU21—4K 13
Swan La. GU17—2F 9
Swan Way. GU13—4G 29
Swift La. GU19—2A 6
Swift Rd. GU9—2F 23
Swift's Clo. GU10—7A 24
Swingate Rd. GU9—2G 27
Swiss Clo. GU19—6D 26
Switchback La. GU10—7D 26
Sycamore Clo. GU17—1D 10
Sycamore Cres. GU13—5H 29
Sycamore Dri. GU10—4D 26
Sycamore Dri. GU12—1F 21
Sycamore Dri. GU16—4D 10
Sycamore Rd. GU14—5B 16
Sycamores, The. GU14—4C 16
Sycamores, The. GU17—1E 8
Sylvan Ridge. GU17—4D 2
Syon Pl. GU14—3C 16

Tadpole La. GU10—7A 18
Talavera Pk. GU11—5K 19
Talbot Clo. GU16—4F 5
Talbot Pl. GU19—2K 5
Talbot Rd. GU24—5C 16
Talgarth Dri. GU14—5C 16
Talisman Clo. RG11—1A 2
Tamworth Dri. GU13—3A 14
Tangier Ct. GU11—6H 19
Tanglewood Ride. GU24—6E 6
Tank Rd. GU15—1J 9
Tarbat Clo. GU15—5G 3
Tarragon La. GU24—3F 15
Tavistock Rd. GU13—2G 29
Tawny Croft. GU15—5H 3
Tay Clo. GU14—1H 15
Tees Clo. GU14—1H 15
Tekels Av. GU15—1C 10
Tekels Pk. GU15—1D 10
Tekels Way. GU15—3D 10
Templar Clo. GU17—5D 2
Ten Acre Wlk. GU10—6C 26
Tenby Rd. GU16—6F 11
Terrace, The. GU15—1K 9
Terrace, The. RG11—1H 3
Tesimond Dri. GU17—3C 28
Thames Clo. GU14—1H 15
Theale Clo. GU15—5G 3
Theobalds Way. GU16—3H 11
Thibet Rd. GU17—5F 3
Thirlmere Clo. GU14—3H 15
Thirlmere Cres. GU13—6H 29
Thirlmere Wlk. GU15—2J 11
Thorn Clo. GU10—6C 26
Thorndown La. GU20—2E 6
Thornfield Grn. GU17—3J 9
Thornhill Rd. GU11—4C 20
Thorn Rd. GU10—5C 26
Thornyhurst Rd. GU16—3F 17
Thorold Rd. GU9—6F 23
Three Stiles Rd. GU9—6C 22
Threshers Corner. GU13—3B 14
Throgmorton Rd. GU17—4C 28
Thundery Hill. GU10—5E 24
Thurbans Rd. GU9—3D 26
Thurston Ho. GU13—2H 29
Thyme Ct. GU14—2F 15
Tichborne Clo. GU15—3E 10
Tichborne Clo. GU17—1G 9
Tichbourne Pl. GU12—1C 24
Tile Barn Clo. GU14—2K 15

Tilford Rd. GU9 & GU10—1G 27
Timber Bank. GU16—1F 17
Timber Clo. GU9—7E 22
Tindal Clo. GU17—7A 2
Tintagel Dri. GU16—5E 10
Toad La. GU17—2H 9
Tockington Ct. GU17—7A 2
Tolpuddle Way. GU17—1C 8
Tomlins Av. GU16—4E 10
Tongham Rd. GU10—5B 24
Tongham Rd. GU12—1C 24
Toplady Pl. GU9—2F 23
Tor Rd. GU9—7C 22
Totford La. GU10—6K 25
Totland Clo. GU14—1K 15
Tottenham Wlk. GU15—4G 3
Tower Hill. GU14—4K 15
Towers Dri. RG11—1E 2
Trafalgar Ct. GU9—1E 26
Trafalgar Way. GU15—2J 9
Trafford Rd. GU16—6C 10
Travis La. GU17—6F 3
Trebor Av. GU10—1G 27
Tredenham Clo. GU14—7B 16
Tree Tops Av. GU15—5F 5
Tregolls Dri. GU14—4B 16
Tremayne Wlk. GU15—2H 11
Trent Clo. GU14—1H 15
Trenton Clo. GU16—4F 11
Tresham Cres. GU17—3C 28
Trimmers Clo. GU9—2E 22
Trimmers Field. GU9—1H 27
Trinity. GU15—3H 3
Trinity Fields. GU9—3D 22
Trinity Hill. GU9—3D 22
Trinity Rd. GU21—5J 13
Trotwood Clo. GU15—2J 9
Troutbeck Wlk. GU15—3J 11
Trunk Rd. GU14—3F 15
Tudor Dri. GU17—2A 8
Tudor Way. GU13—7K 29
Turf Hill Rd. GU15—5E 4
Turner Pl. GU15—7G 3
Turnstone End. GU17—3D 28
Turnville Clo. GU18—4B 6
Tuscam Way. GU15—2J 9
Tweed Clo. GU14—1H 15
Tweedsmuir Clo. GU14—4G 15
Twelve Acre Cres. GU14—2G 15
Tweseldown Rd. GU13—4A 18
Twyford Clo. GU14—4E 26
Twynham Rd. GU15—1B 10
Tyne Clo. GU14—1H 15

Ullswater Av. GU14—4H 15
Ullswater Clo. GU9—3D 22
Ullswater Clo. GU18—4C 6
Ulswater Rd. GU18—4C 6
Underhill La. GU14—1H 15
Underwood Av. GU12—7D 20
Union Clo. GU15—3H 3
Union Rd. GU9—7F 23
Union Rd. GU16—6J 11
Union St. GU14—6K 19
Union St. GU14—3K 15
Union St. GU24—7B 12
Union Ter. GU11—6K 19
Updown Hill. GU20—1E 6
Upland Rd. GU15—6C 4
Uplands Clo. GU17—5E 2
Uplands Rd. GU9—1H 27
Up. Bourne La. GU10—5D 26
Up. Bourne Vale. GU10—5D 26
Up. Broadmoor Rd. RG11—1F 3
Up. Charles St. GU15—7B 4
Up. Chobham Rd. GU15—3F 11
Up. Church La. GU9—7E 22
Up. College Ride. GU15—5D 4
Up. Elms Rd. GU11—7K 19
Up. Gordon Rd. GU15—1C 10
Up. Hale Rd. GU9—2D 22
Up. Old Pk. La. GU9—4C 22
Up. Park Rd. GU15—1C 10
Up. Pinewood Rd. GU12—5J 21
Up. St Michael's Rd
—1K 23

Up. South View. GU9—6F 23
Upper St. GU13—2J 29
Up. Union St. GU11—6K 19
Up. Union Ter. GU11—6K 19
Up. Verran Rd. GU15—3C 10
Upper Way. GU9—2D 26
Up. Weybourne La. GU9—1G 23
Upton Clo. GU14—4C 16

Vale Clo. GU10—6F 27
Vale Rd. GU12—1F 21
Vale Rd. GU15—2K 9
Vale Wood Dri. GU10—6G 27
Valley End Rd. GU24—1H 7
Valley La. GU14—4F 27
Valley Rd. GU16—6F 11
Valroy Clo. GU15—7C 4
Varney Clo. GU14—2H 15
Velmead Clo. GU13—1A 18
Velmead Rd. GU13—4K 29
Ventnor Ter. GU12—7B 20
Verne, The. GU15—3H 3
Vernon Ct. GU9—7D 22
Veronica Dri. GU13—6G 29
Verran Rd. GU15—3C 10
Vesey Clo. GU14—2K 15
Vicarage Gdns. GU13—7J 29
Vicarage Hill. GU9 & GU10
—3G 27
Vicarage La. GU9—7E 22
(Farnham)
Vicarage La. GU9—3G 27
(The Bourne)
Vicarage La. GU9—2F 23
(Upper Hale)
Vicarage La. GU17—2E 28
(Blackwater)
Vicarage La. GU17—2H 9
(Yateley)
Vicarage Rd. GU17—2D 28
(Yateley)
Vicarage Rd. GU19—2H 5
Victoria Av. GU15—1K 9
Victoria Ct. GU13—2J 29
Victoria Ct. GU14—4K 5
Victoria Dri. GU17—2F 9
Victoria Gdns. GU13—2J 29
Victoria Hill. GU13—2H 29
Victoria Rd. GU9—7F 23
Victoria Rd. GU11—6K 19
Victoria Rd. GU13—2H 29
Victoria Rd. GU14—3K 15
Victoria Rd. GU15—4H 3
Victoria Rd. GU21—4K 13
Vigo La. GU17—4E 28
Village Way. GU17—6A 2
Vine Clo. GU10—6D 26
Vine Clo. GU11—2K 19
Vine Ho. Clo. GU16—4F 17
Vine St. GU11—7K 19
Vine Way. GU10—5D 26
Virginia Gdns. GU14—5B 16
Vivian Clo. GU13—2A 18
Vulcan Clo. GU14—6D 2
Vulcan Way. GU17—6E 2

Wadham. GU15—4J 3
Waggoners Hollow. GU19
—3K 5
Wagon Yd. GU9—7E 22
Wakefords Copse. GU13—5A 18
Wakefords Pk. GU13—5A 18
Waldorf Heights. GU17—3G 9
Walker's Ridge. GU15—2D 10
Wallington Rd. GU15—4F 5
Walls Ct. GU16—7D 10
Walmer Clo. GU16—7F 11
Walnut Clo. GU17—2A 8
Waltham Rd. GU15—4G 3
Walton Clo. GU13—3J 29
Wandle Clo. GU17—2A 8
Wansdyke Clo. GU16—6E 10
Wantage Rd. GU15—5G 3
Warbury La. GU21—3K 13
Wardle Clo. GU19—2K 5

Wargrove Dri. GU15—5G 3
Warren Clo. GU13—1A 18
Warren Clo. GU17—5D 2
Warren M. GU11—1H 23
Warren Rise. GU16—4D 10
Warren, The. GU9—1H 23
Warren, The. GU11—7J 19
Warren Way. GU21—5K 13
Warwick Clo. GU11—1B 24
Warwick Clo. GU15—3G 11
Warwick Rd. GU12—7F 17
Wasdale Clo. GU15—3G 3
Watchetts Dri. GU15—4B 10
Watchetts Lake Clo. GU15
—3C 10
Watchetts Rd. GU15—2A 10
Watchmoor Pk. GU15—3K 9
Watchmoor Rd. GU15—2K 9
Waterers Rise. GU21—4K 13
Waterhouse Mead. GU15—6G 3
Water La. GU9—5H 23
Water La. GU13—7G 29
Water La. GU14—7K 9
Water La. GU24—3J 7
Waterloo Pl. RG11—1E 2
Waterloo Rd. GU12—7B 20
Waterloo Rd. RG11—1D 2
(Crowthorne)
Waterside Ct. GU13—4A 14
Watery La. GU24—4K 7
Watts Rd. GU14—2J 15
Waverley Av. GU13—1J 29
Waverley Clo. GU9—2H 23
Waverley Clo. GU15—2E 10
Waverley Dri. GU12—2F 21
Waverley Dri. GU15—1E 10
Waverley Gdns. GU12—2F 21
Waverley La. GU9—7G 23
Waverley Rd. GU14—4C 16
Waverley Rd. GU19—2K 5
Wayman Rd. GU14—6H 9
Waynflete La. GU9—7C 22
Ways End. GU15—2D 10
Weavers Grn. GU9—3C 26
Weavers Yd. GU9—7E 22
Webb Clo. GU19—4K 5
Weir Av. GU14—4K 15
Weir Clo. GU14—4K 15
Welbeck Clo. GU14—4J 15
Weldon Clo. GU13—3A 18
Well Clo. GU21—2H 13
Wellesley Clo. GU12—1E 20
Wellesley Clo. GU19—2H 5
Wellesley Garden. GU9—2F 23
Wellesley Rd. GU15—1G 19
Wellesley Rd. GU12—2E 20
(in two parts)
Wellesley Rd. GU14—7G 15
Wellesly Dri. RG11—1B 2
Wellington Av. GU11—6H 19
Wellington Av. GU13—5A 14
Wellington Centre. GU11
—6K 19
Wellington Clo. GU17—5F 3
Wellington Gdns. GU11—7J 19
Wellingtonia Av. GU15—1J 11
Wellingtonia Av. RG11—1A 2
Wellington La. GU9—2G 23
Wellington Rd. GU17—5E 2
Wellington Rd. RG11—1F 3
(Crowthorne)
Wellington Ter. GU11—6K 19
Wellington Ter. GU17—5F 3
Wells Cotts. GU9—3B 26
Wendover Dri. GU16—3H 11
Wensleydale Dri. GU15—1J 11
Wensley Dri. GU13—1K 29
Wentworth Clo. GU9—3J 23
Wentworth Clo. GU12—1F 21
Wentworth Cres. GU12—2F 21
Wessex Pl. GU9—1F 27
West Av. GU9—3G 23
Westbourne Rd. GU15—6H 3
Westbury Av. GU13—7C 14
Westbury Clo. GU13—7B 14
Westbury Gdns. GU13—7C 14
West Clo. GU9—2G 23

W. End Gro. GU9—7D 22
Westerdale Dri. GU16—3G 11
Western Rd. GU11—7H 19
Westfield Ct. GU13—2K 29
Westfield Rd. GU15—4A 10
W. Fryerne. GU17—5A 2
W. Glade. GU14—3G 15
W. Green. GU17—2D 28
W. Heath Rd. GU14—3J 15
W. Hill Clo. GU24—7J 13
Westland Ct. GU14—4J 15
Westmead. GU14—3A 16
Westminster Clo. GU13—1K 29
Westmorland Dri. GU15—3G 11
Weston Gro. GU19—3A 6
Westover Rd. GU15—6A 4
West Rd. GU14—7A 10
West Rd. GU15—1C 10
West St. GU9—1C 26
Westwood Rd. GU20—1D 6
Wetherby Gdns. GU14—7B 16
Weybank Clo. GU9—7F 23
Weybourne Rd. GU9 & GU11
—4H 23
Weybridge Mead. GU17—6B 2
Wey Clo. GU12—7F 21
Wey Clo. GU15—1A 10
Weydon Hill Clo. GU9—2E 26
Weydon Hill Rd. GU9—2E 26
Weydon La. GU9—3C 26
Weydon Mill Clo. GU9—1E 26
Weyside. GU9—7F 23
Weywood La. GU9—2H 23
Wharfenden Way. GU16—1E 16
Wharf Rd. GU12—4F 21
Wharf Rd. GU16—1E 16
Wharf Way. GU16—1F 17
Whetstone Rd. GU14—3F 15
Whin Holt. GU13—5K 29
Whins Clo. GU15—2A 10
Whins Dri. GU15—2A 10
Whistler Gro. GU15—7G 3
Whitchurch Clo. GU11—3C 24
White Acres Rd. GU16—3C 16
Whitebeam Gdns. GU14—4F 15
White Cottage Clo. GU16—3G 23
Whitehill Clo. GU15—6C 4
White Ho. Gdns. GU17—2E 28
White Ho. Wlk. GU9—2G 23
White La. GU12 & GU10—7H 21
White Lion Way. GU17—6A 2
White Post La. GU10—5D 26
White Rd. GU15—7J 3
White Rose La. GU9—3F 23
Whites Rd. GU14—6D 16
Whitley Rd. GU17—2A 8
Whitmoor Rd. GU19—2A 6
Whitmore Clo. GU15—5G 3
Whitmore Grn. GU9—3H 23
Whittle Clo. GU17—4D 2
Whittle Cres. GU14—7J 9
Whyte Av. GU12—1C 24
Wicket Hill. GU10—4D 26
Wickham Clo. GU15—5H 29
Wickham Ct. GU13—5H 29
Wickham Pl. GU13—5H 29
Wickham Rd. GU13—5H 29
Wickham Rd. GU15—5D 4
Wilcot Clo. GU24—3H 13
Wilcot Gdns. GU24—3H 13
Wilderness Rd. GU16—4D 10
Wilders Clo. GU16—3D 10
Wildwood Gdns. GU17—5E 28
William Farthing Clo. GU11
—6K 19
Williams Way. GU13—6B 14
Willington Clo. GU15—6H 3
Willow Clo. GU16—3D 16
Willow Ct. GU12—1F 21
Willow Cres. GU14—7A 10
Willowford. GU17—7A 2
Willow Grn. GU24—7G 7
Willow La. GU12—2E 9
Willow Pk. GU12—6E 20
Willow Rd. GU24—7G 7
Willows End. GU17—5E 2

Willows, The. GU18—4E 6
Willow Way. GU9—3G 23
Willow Way. GU12—1D 24
Willow Way. GU17—4C 2
Wilmot Way. GU15—3E 10
Wilson Rd. GU12—7C 20
Wilson Rd. GU14—4J 15
Wilton Ct. GU14—4C 16
Wilton Rd. GU15—3A 10
Wimbledon Clo. GU15—4E 4
Wimbledon Rd. GU15—4E 4
Winchester Rd. GU12—5F 21
Winchester St. GU14—7B 16
Winchester Way. GU17—7F 3
Windermere Clo. GU14—4H 15
Windermere Rd. GU18—4C 6
Windermere Wlk. GU15—1J 11
Windermere Way. GU9—3D 22
Winding Wood Dri. GU15
—2G 11
Windle Clo. GU20—1E 6
Windlesham Rd. GU24—2H 7
(Chobham)
Windlesham Rd. GU24—5F 7
(West End)
Windmill Field. GU20—1D 6
Windmill Hill. GU12—7B 20
Windmill Rd. GU12—7B 20
Windrush Heights. GU17—5D 2
Windsor Ct. GU13—2J 29
Windsor Cres. GU9—3E 22
Windsor Ride. GU15 & RG11
—5K 3
Windsor Rd. GU14—6C 16
Windsor Rd. GU24—1K 7
Windsor Way. GU11—6A 20
Windsor Way. GU16—6E 10
Wingfield Gdns. GU13—3J 11
Wings Rd. GU9—2E 22
Winston Clo. GU16—1E 16
Winston Wlk. GU14—4F 27
Winterbourne Wlk. GU16
—6E 10
Winton Cres. GU17—1A 8
Winton Rd. GU9—6G 23
Winton Rd. GU11—7K 19
Wishmoor Clo. GU15—5D 4
Wishmoor Rd. GU15—5D 4
Wistaria La. GU17—4E 28
Withy Clo. GU18—4D 6
Wittmead Rd. GU16—3E 16
Woburn Av. GU14—3C 16
Woburn Clo. GU16—7J 11
Wokingham Rd. GU11 & GU17
—1B 2
Wolfe Rd. GU12—7B 20
Wolseley Rd. GU11—7K 19
Woodbine Clo. GU17—6F 3
Woodbourne. GU9—2H 23
Woodbourne Dri. GU17—7A 2
Woodbridge Dri. GU15—6C 4
Woodbridge Rd. GU17—1E 8
Woodcock Dri. GU24—2K 7
Woodcock La. GU24—2J 7
Woodcote Grn. GU13—3G 29
Woodcot Gdns. GU14—3G 15
Woodcott Ter. GU11—1C 24
Woodcut Rd. GU10—4C 26
Wood End. GU14—4C 16
Wood End. RG11—1C 2
Woodend Rd. GU16—7H 11
Woodgate. GU13—4B 14
Woodland Dri. GU10—4E 26
Woodlands. GU13—1J 29
Woodlands. GU17—3A 8
Woodlands Av. GU9—2J 23
Woodlands Clo. GU13—3F 21
Woodlands Clo. GU17—5H 9
Woodlands Clo. GU15—4J 3
Woodlands La. GU20—1E 6
Woodlands Rd. GU14—1G 15
Woodlands Rd. GU15—1A 10
Woodlands Wlk. GU17—5H 9
Wood La. GU10—5G 25
Wood La. GU13—6B 14
Wood La. GU14—4K 15
Wood Leigh. GU13—3K 29

Woodman Ct. GU13—3J 29
Woodpecker Clo. GU10—1A 22
Wood Rd. GU9—2F 23
Wood Rd. GU15—5A 10
Woodside. GU15—6J 3
Woodside. GU17—4F 9
Woodside Rd. GU9—2H 23
Woodstocks. GU14—1B 16
Woodstock Ter. GU11—1C 20
Wood St. GU12—2F 21
Woodville Clo. GU17—1E 8
Wood Way. GU15—1A 10
Woollards Rd. GU12—4G 21
Woolmead Rd. GU9—6F 23
Woolmead, The. GU9—6F 23

Woolmead Wlk. GU9—6F 23
(off East St.)
Worcester Clo. GU14—7A 10
Wordsworth Av. GU17—4D 28
Worsley Rd. GU16—6D 10
Wrecclesham Hill. GU10
—5A 26
Wrecclesham Rd. GU9—3C 26
Wren Clo. GU17—3D 28
Wren Ct. GU12—5G 21
Wren Way. GU14—7J 9
Wychelm Rd. GU18—5D 6
Wychwood Clo. GU12—6E 20
Wychwood Pl. GU15—4G 5
Wyke Av. GU12—5J 21

Wyke Bldgs. GU12—5J 21
Wykeham Rd. GU9—6F 23
Wyke La. GU12—5J 21
Wymering Ct. GU14—4C 16
Wyndham Clo. GU17—6A 2
Wyndham St. GU12—7B 20
Wynfields. GU16—4E 16

Yale Clo. GU15—3J 3
Yateley Centre. GU17—3E 28
Yateley Rd. GU17—5C 2
Yatesbury Clo. GU9—3C 26
Yaverland Dri. GU19—3J 5
Yellowcress Dri. GU24—3H 13

Yeomans Clo. GU10—1E 24
Yeomans Clo. GU14—2K 15
Yeomans Way. GU15—1D 10
Yeoman Ter. GU21—4K 13
(off Queen's Rd.)
Yeovil Clo. GU14—6C 16
Yeovil Rd. GU14—6D 16
Yeovil Rd. GU15—4G 3
Yetminster Rd. GU14—6C 16
Yew Tree Clo. GU14—4F 15
Yew Tree Wlk. GU16—5E 10
Yockley Clo. GU15—2J 11
Yolland Clo. GU9—2F 23
York Cres. GU11—7J 19
York Rd. GU9—2F 27

York Rd. GU11—7J 19
York Rd. GU12—5F 21
York Rd. GU14—6B 16
York Rd. GU15—6C 4
Yorktown Rd. GU17 & GU15
—5D 2
York Way. GU17—5E 2
Youlden Clo. GU15—1F 11
Youlden Dri. GU15—1F 11
Youngs Dri. GU12—6E 20

Zinnia Dri. GU24—3H 13

Every possible care has been taken to ensure that the information given in this publication is accurate and whilst the publishers would be grateful to learn of any errors, they regret they cannot accept any responsibility for loss thereby caused.

The representation on the maps of a road, track or footpath is no evidence of the existence of a right of way.

The Grid on this map is the National Grid taken from the Ordnance Survey map with the permission of the Controller of Her Majesty's Stationery Office.

Copyright of Geographers' A-Z Map Co. Ltd.

No reproduction by any method whatsoever of any part of this publication is permitted without the prior consent of the copyright owners.